WARLEY WOODS · SMETHWICK

Centenary of The People's Park

An Illustrated History

PRODUCED BY

Warley Woods Community Trust

EDITORIAL TEAM

ANDREW MAXAM
ALAN REYNOLDS
DELIA GARRETT
STEVE CEMM

FOREWORDS BY

CARL CHINN
JULIE WALTERS
COLIN BUCHANAN

Front Cover: **Aerial view of Warley Woods, park and golf course, from the south west: 2001**
Rear Cover: (Upper) **The front entrance to Warley Abbey c. 1912**
(Lower) **The golf professional, A. J. Padgham, on the 7th green on Warley Golf Course, 1930's**

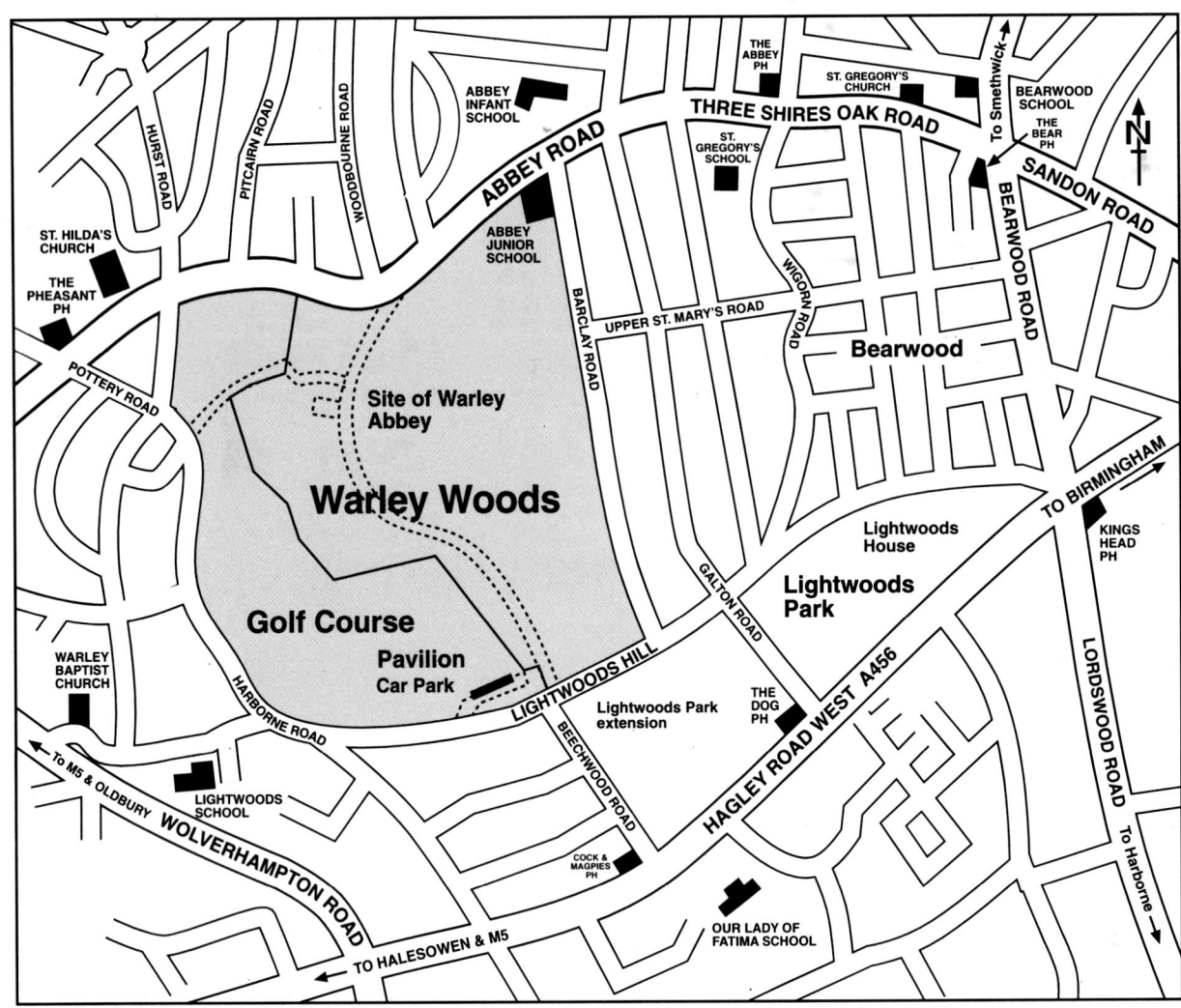

1 Warley Woods and its surroundings.

ISBN 0 9543913 1 4

First published 2006 © Crown Cards, Smethwick, West Midlands.

Intellectual rights in illustrative material in this book remain the property of those to whom ownership has been attributed.
All rights reserved. No part of this publication may be reproduced, stored in a retrieval system, or transmitted in any form or by any means, electronic, mechanical, photocopying, recording or otherwise, without the prior permission of the copyright holder. Warley Woods Community Trust has asserted its right under the Copyright, Designs and Patents Act, 1988 to be identified as the author of this book.
Every effort has asserted to trace and acknowledge copyright holders to reproduce their material. Sincere apologies are offered where this has proved unsuccessful.

Printed and bound by Adlard Print & Reprographics Ltd., Ruddington, Nottingham NG11 6HH

2 The opening of Warley Woods as a public park: June 9th 1906.

3 Warley Woods Community Trust's Picnic in the Park.

Foreword by Julie Walters OBE

Growing up in Bearwood in the fifties and sixties, Warley Woods was always a special, and slightly mysterious place for me.
So, when I heard about the plans to restore the Woods, and that it was to be run by a Community Trust made up of Smethwick people, I was pleased to become a Patron.
A park, even a beautiful one like this, is no more than trees, paths, grass and railings – it's the people who use it that bring it alive: people meeting up, walking the dog, playing golf, falling in love, having great ideas, daydreaming or kicking a football. And it's about people who care enough to get up off their backsides – I was told I couldn't say "arses" – and work together to help bring this special place back to life.
Happy 100th Birthday, Warley Woods
(Do you get a telegram from the Queen?)

Foreword by Colin Buchanan

Having lived for thirteen years in the social desert that is London, I decided to become an adoptive Brummie back in 1997, and eventually came to live by Warley Woods. In a time when so many of our city spaces are being concreted over and built upon, it was a real joy to find such a green oasis, not just on my doorstep, but right at the heart of the community.
The Woods and Meadow benefit us all in so many ways from simply being a pleasant place to walk, to exercising (both human and animal), golfing, sledging or just lazing in the sunshine. They also perform an educational function for many of our local schoolchildren. Most of all though, they provide a focal point for all the people who live in the area. This is most clearly borne out by thousands who turn out to the annual Picnic In The Park.
After years of neglect, the running and maintenance of the Woods is now in the hands of the Community Trust, who have already made great strides since assuming control from the Council. Let us hope that The Peoples Park, as it was originally dubbed in 1906, will continue to thrive for the next hundred years and beyond.

Foreword
by
Professor Carl Chinn,
MBE, PhD

One hundred years ago, Alexander Macomb Chance, the great Smethwick industrialist belonging to the world famous firm of glassmakers, campaigned to secure a vital and historic open space for the folk of Warley, Smethwick, Oldbury and the nearby neighbourhoods of Birmingham. Known today as Warley Woods, from the first this was the People's Park, as Chance wanted it to be. The people flocked to support Chance's initiative and as he declared at the opening ceremony, "never was there a park in the Midlands before that was paid for directly by the money of the people."

Owned for many years by Birmingham City Council, Warley Woods now belongs to the people in the broadest and most democratic of senses through a community trust. That Trust is committed to honouring the vision of Chance and those ordinary folk who backed him. It is as committed to protecting a landscape that has been fashioned carefully and sensitively for over one thousand years. Medieval farmers have left traces of their ridges and furrows. Humphry Repton, the celebrated landscape architect who was employed by the Galtons in the late eighteenth century, created contrived views that slowly unfold, whilst George Bretherick, the park superintendent from 1906-1935, laid out exotic flowerbeds.

All that and more was at risk at the turn of the twenty first century. A new campaign was needed, from which arose the Warley Woods Community Trust. The Trust holds fast to the vision and commitment of Chance and to the determination of the local folk who saved the park for the people a century ago. I am honoured to be patron of of such a sensitive and valuable organisation that cherishes Warley Woods; and I pay tribute both to its vital work and to its publication of this evocative book. I feel certain that Alexander Macomb Chance would have been as proud of the Trust and its achievements as am I.

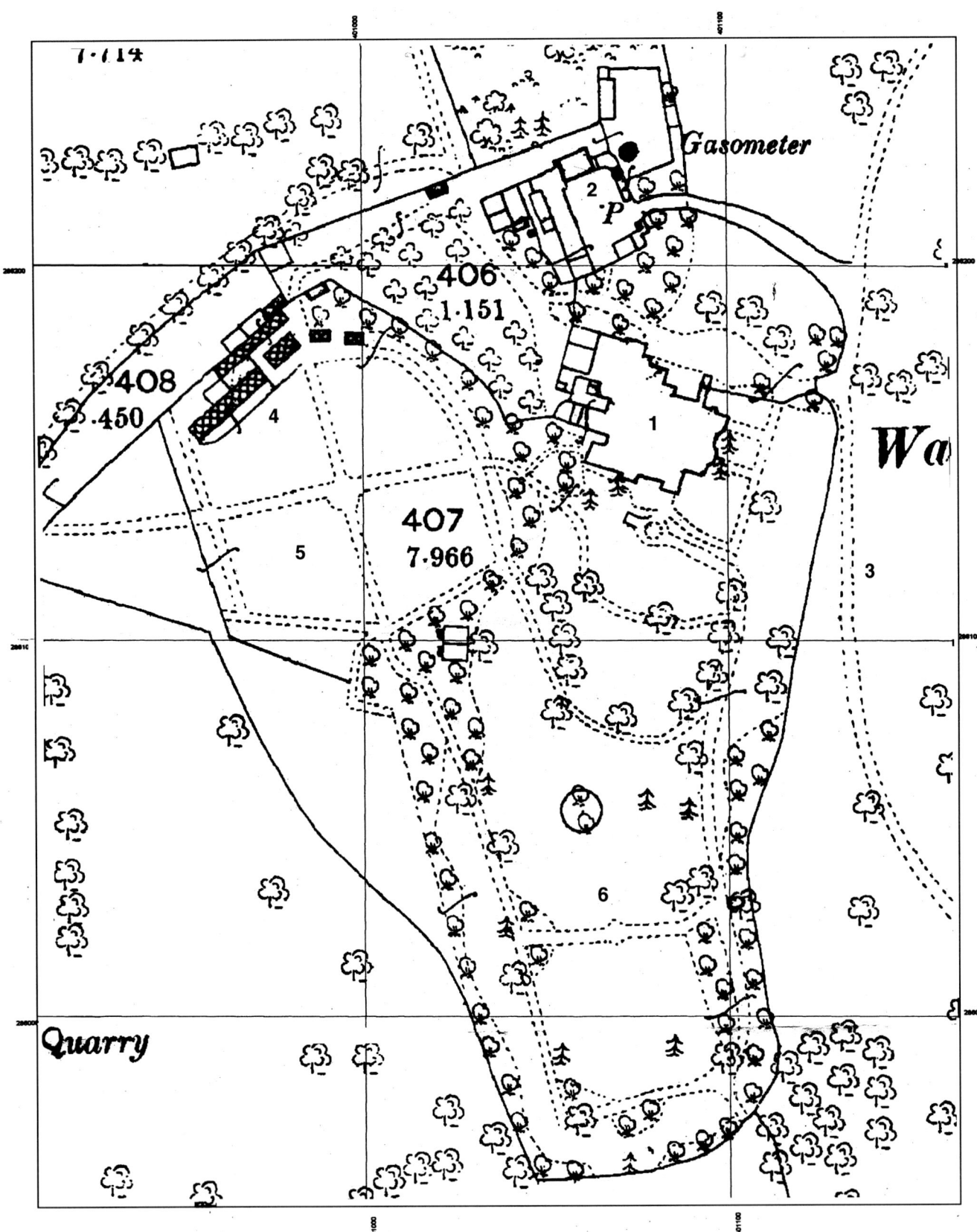

4 An extract from an early edition OS map c.1880 showing the Abbey and its immediate surroundings.
1. Warley Abbey; 2. Stables and gasometer; 3. Main Driveway; 4. Glasshouses; 5. Kitchen garden;
6. Winter garden and arboretum.

Preface

2006 marks the centenary of the opening of Warley Woods as a public park. The park is of particular interest as it is Listed [Grade 2] by English Heritage, on account of its survival as a landscape substantially designed and laid out in the early nineteenth century by Humphry Repton. This combination of a Repton-designed, free-to-access landscape, incorporated into a public park and golf course, and run by a community trust made up entirely of local volunteers is, to our knowledge, unique in Britain. Warley Woods Community Trust therefore felt that the centenary should not be allowed to pass without some form of commemoration and celebration. This book is in many ways the focus of our energies, for although there will be a number of special events taking place throughout the year, we felt there needed also to be a permanent and lasting record. In this book we are hoping to tell something of the history of the site, not only through words, but also by sharing with you as many images of the park, woods, golf course and the immediately surrounding streets, as space will permit.

Warley Woods lies about 6 kilometres [4 miles] west of Birmingham city centre. The site is approximately 40 hectares [100 acres] in extent, and is roughly square in shape, with each side about 650 metres long. The total perimeter length, for those who like to walk or run round it, is 2700 metres [1.7 miles]. The edges of the park are aligned almost exactly with the points of the compass: to the east lies Barclay Road; to the south Lightwoods Hill, Harborne Road to the west and on the north side Abbey Road. The land is high up, reaching 230 metres above sea level [around 750 feet] by the water tower. There are extensive views in most directions, particularly to the north and east, towards Cannock Chase and Charnwood Forest respectively. Head east from the water tower and the next highest ground is in the Ural mountains of Russia, approximately 2000 miles away. The underlying geology of the park is bunter pebble, a free draining sandy pebbly soil, which explains why the stream through the meadow has only ever run occasionally, and also why the golf course remains playable in the wettest of weather. The whole site is divided up very roughly into thirds, split between the golf course, meadow and the woodland. There are around 4000 trees across the site, of a variety of ages and types, though the most common species are beech and oak.

We do not pretend that this will be an exhaustive or definitive history of Warley Woods; instead, we have aimed for a reflective look back at key events and decisions that have made the park what it is today. We have deliberately set out not only to report facts, but also in places to draw out comparisons, and to offer thoughts on events and actions. Any opinions expressed are those of the editorial team alone, and do not necessarily imply endorsement from Warley Woods Community Trust, Warley Woods Golf Club, Birmingham City Council or Sandwell Metropolitan Borough Council. Those who wish to learn more of the details of the site's fascinating past, and of the lives of the people who shaped it, particularly in the period before the creation of the public park in 1906, are strongly recommended to follow these up through David Yates's excellent publications **The History of the Warley Hall Estate** and **A Place in Time, a History of Warley Hall, Warley Abbey and Warley Park**. We are greatly indebted to David for allowing us to raid his extensive back catalogue of knowledge, and for acting as our 'truth or myth' filter.

Our other key collaborator, without whom the book would not have been possible, is local publisher Andrew Maxam. Many of the photographic images used in this book have been drawn from Andrew's encyclopaedic collection of local postcard views, supplemented by other photographs that Andrew has sourced for us. Throughout, our aim has been to select wherever possible illustrations that are unseen or unpublished, in order to present some fresh, and hopefully thought-provoking insights into the history of this unique site.

We are also grateful to Sandwell Council's Community Archive at Smethwick Library, and to Peter Drake of Birmingham Central Library's Local Studies section for his assistance and co-operation in helping to locate images, and for allowing us to use them. Other views have been provided by the work of the late Joe Russell, Steve Cemm, Alan and Gail Reynolds, as well as those drawn from the Trust's own archive.

Finally, while putting this book together has been something of a labour of love for the editorial team, it has also been an eye-opener to us. We had assumed that the complete history of the site was out there, somewhere, chronicled and recorded, and that our job was simply to research, uncover and plagiarise. Up to a point, that has been true, certainly in respect of some of the important phases in the evolution of the site. Repton's Red Book, for example, the formation of the public park in 1906 and the demolition of the abbey in 1957 are accurately and comprehensively archived. Where we have had more difficulty is in defining with precision some of the more recent history of the site, particularly the years of decline from the 1960's onwards. We hope that the publication of this book will prompt people to come forward with additional material, photos and recollections, to help us fill in these gaps in our knowledge.

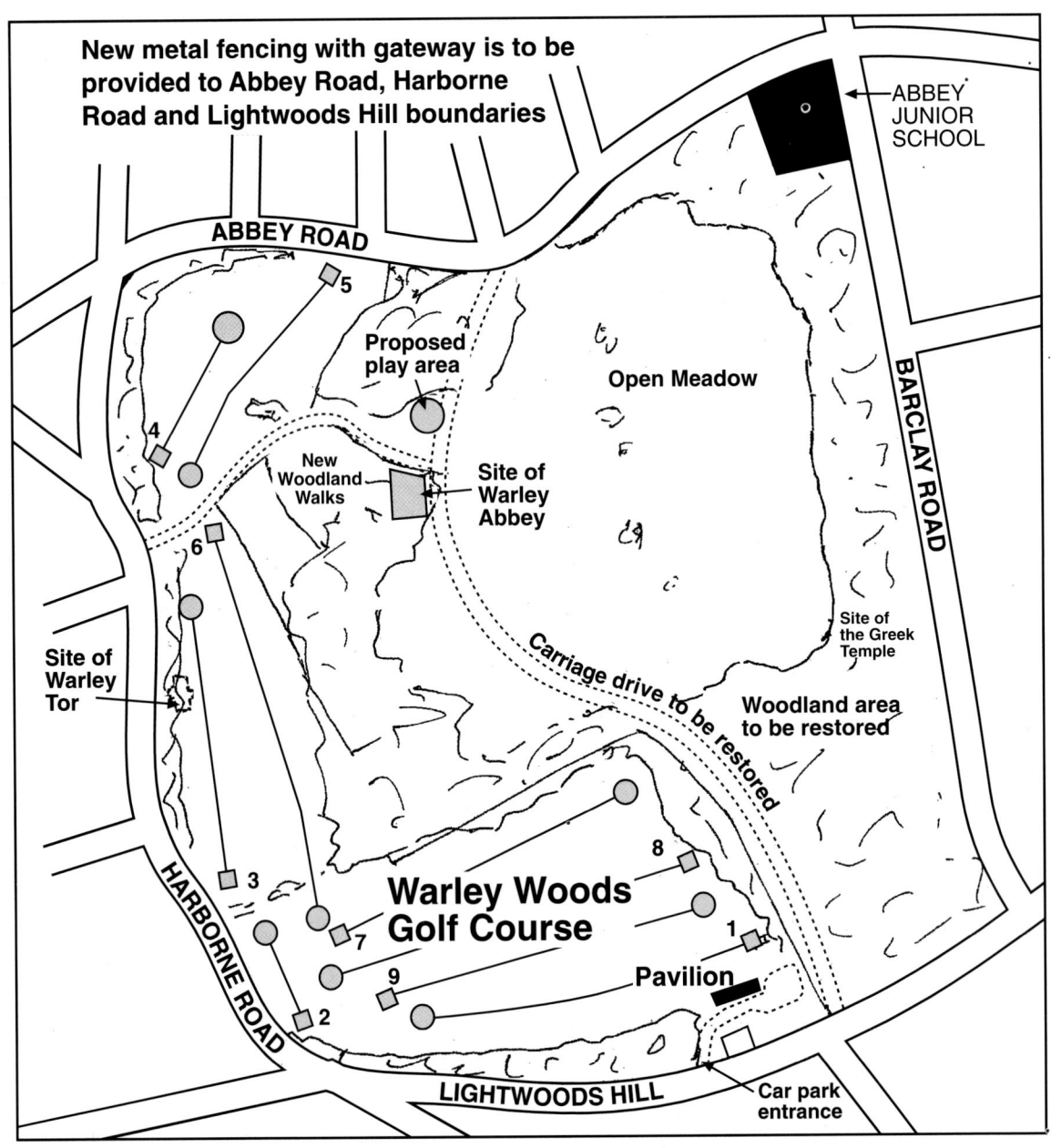

5 Warley Woods, showing key features - past, present and future.

Repton, Galton and the building of Warley Abbey

The earliest known reference to the Warley Hall Estate occurred in 1561. The history of the estate from the middle ages right up to the purchase of the estate by Galton, in 1792, is covered, in great detail, in David Yates's comprehensive history **The History of the Warley Hall Estate**.

Our story begins with Samuel Galton Junior, who was one of Birmingham's most renowned and influential businessmen, a gunmaker and a Quaker. From the early 1780's he lived at Great Barr Hall and in 1792 acquired Warley, for £7,300. The estate was based on Warley Hall, and its associated farm, which were situated close to where Grove Road now runs. However, the landholding of the estate extended eastwards from Bleakhouse Road across the whole of Warley Woods, as far as Wigorn Road.

The estate contained Warley Tor, a circular summer house with an observation platform above, and a single room each side at ground level, giving it the shape, in plan form, of a wing nut. It is not known for certain whether the Tor existed when Galton purchased the estate, or whether he had it built around 1792. We are not even sure of its precise location, as no accurate plans or drawings exist, and successive archaeological surveys have so far failed to locate any remains.

We can be reasonably certain that it was built high up on, or very close to, what is now the third fairway of the golf course, between Grove Road and Lenwade Road. We also believe that from the viewing platform it would have been possible to see the Galtons' home at Great Barr, approximately 11 kilometres [7 miles] away. Around this time, the line of Harborne Road was diverted westwards, so that the Tor became part of the landscaped park.

Two years after purchasing the estate, in 1794, Galton commissioned the fashionable landscape architect Humphry Repton to draw up plans for landscaping part of the estate, in a style that was fitting for a prosperous country gentleman. Initially there was no intention of replacing Warley Hall with a new house; Repton merely suggested this as he thought a classical house would enhance his proposed parkland at some later date. The park was to be created as an investment, and as a business statement, for Galton wished to portray the image of a man who could afford a large estate **and** turn part of it into pleasure grounds. Repton had established a reputation for remodelling existing landscapes of fields, plantations, hedges, streams and woodlands into natural looking parkland settings for great houses. He was therefore in his element here. His plans would follow particular rules and principles, and his recommendations would be presented to clients in his trademark Red Book.

To convey his ideas, and win over his clients, Repton would not only use words, but also include watercolour sketches of the site as existing, together with a series of transparent overlays showing exactly how his proposals would look when complete. In terms of presentation, this was considered slick and cutting-edge for the 1790's, and these sales techniques almost certainly helped win him many commissions, and established his reputation as a successful and much sought-after landscape designer.

When Repton first visited Warley he would have seen a wooded rural landscape, with rolling hills, enclosed fields, copses, areas of woodland and occasional farmsteads, connected by narrow, winding and sometimes steep lanes and tracks; imagine the present-day countryside of North Worcestershire, around Clent or Romsley, for example. He would have seen the potential offered by the broad sweep of what is now the meadow, with plantations of trees and the skyline beyond. He would have spotted the chance to create an impression of space and distance within a relatively confined area. Here, he could conjure up for his client Samuel Galton the perfect image of a country gentleman's rural home, apparently set deep within boundless countryside, but in fact only a short distance from his factory in Birmingham.

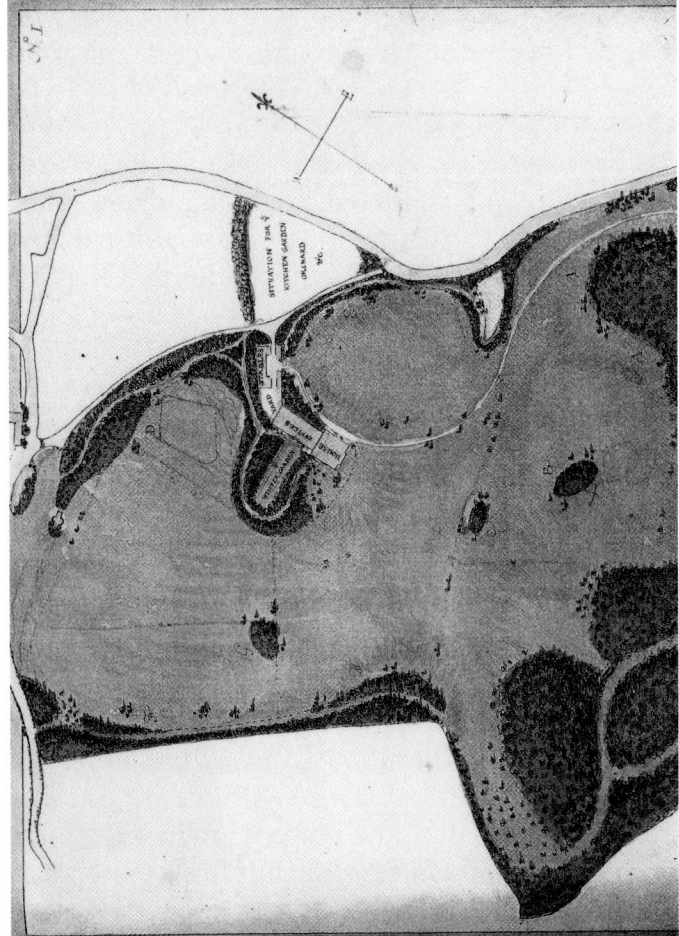

6 1792 plan of the pre-Repton landscape, with proposed changes overlaid.

7 Part of Repton's Red Book plans, showing the proposed classical house and sweeping driveway c.1794: note the misplaced north point.

8 · 9 Front and rear views of proposal to extend and improve Warley Tor, designed by Robert Lugar, published in his 1828 book; no evidence exists that these works were ever carried out.

In suggesting a site for the house, Repton carefully considered the whole range of views both towards, and away from, the building. He also studied the forces of nature and the rhythm of the seasons. Light and shade, the tracking of the sun at different times of year, the seasonal nature of leaf cover and protection from the prevailing westerly wind were all thought about. Interestingly, given this attention to detail, his earliest plans for the park showed the direction of "north" wrong by about 50 degrees. Despite this error, in every other sense his Red Book for Warley Park, produced in 1795, was a triumph of both substance and presentation, and provided Galton with a well-considered set of proposals.

Repton set out in his rules of landscaping that the house should be approached through woodland, and first glimpsed across the head of an open valley, through which a stream would run. The main drive from the north would have wound its way down through the trees from where the Abbey School retaining wall ends, burst out into the meadow, swept majestically across a small bridge over the stream and curved its way around and up to the house. This would have given Galton's guests ample time to admire his elegant estate from several angles as they gradually drew near.

He was also insistent that the extent of the estate should appear limitless from the house, by ensuring that boundaries were set beyond the horizon. This was in order to create a sense of spaciousness, and conjure up an impression that the park was several times its actual size. Repton was clearly successful in promoting this deceit; 200 years on, today's park users often refer to the feeling of being in a much larger open space, somewhere it is possible to 'lose yourself', away from the noise of traffic and the pressures of urban life.

10 Humphry Repton at work – from an 18th century engraving.

Also, in seeking perfection in landscape composition, Repton would try to filter out, eliminate or disguise those features he considered jarring or inappropriate; farms, for example. He believed passionately that although a country gentleman could run a farm, he should not be seen to be a farmer, and that farms therefore should be kept out of sight of a gentleman's residence. From Warley, it would have been possible to see three different farms: Slatch House Farm stood beyond Abbey Road, nearly opposite the school; Lightwoods Farm occupied the site of the golf compound, off Lightwoods Hill; and Warley Hall Farm was beyond Harborne Road, near Grove Road. Where possible, he planted additional trees or shrubs around the estate to screen or hide these farm buildings. However, in the case of Lightwoods Farm, he had built a mock-Grecian, or Doric temple, on the eastern side of the meadow, set into a specially sculpted woodland recess. This was intended to be a folly, or eyecatcher, visible across the meadow from the abbey and drawing the eye away from the farmstead beyond.

One might imagine that the submission of the Red Book for Warley would have been followed closely by a period of frantic building activity and associated landscape remodelling. In the event, little, if anything, happened for a number of years, and Samuel continued to live at Great Barr Hall with his family, including son Hubert, born 1789.

By 1817, Hubert Galton was living at Hockley Abbey in Birmingham; his growing family made this home increasingly overcrowded, and in looking around for a new house, he considered expanding and rebuilding Warley Tor. With this in mind, Hubert approached the eminent Scottish architect Robert Lugar and commissioned him to draw up plans to alter and enlarge the Tor. These plans, shown in Lugar's 1828 book 'Villa Architecture' came to nothing; however Hubert clearly liked his approach, in which he proposed transforming this ugly duckling of a 'mere round building without dressing of any kind' into an elegant classical swan. For whatever reason, Hubert abandoned the idea of enlarging the Tor, and in 1818 he re-engaged Lugar to design a new home elsewhere in the grounds of the estate, which was to be funded through a gift of £1000 from his father. The Tor subsequently fell into disuse, and it was probably demolished by about 1850.

Hubert Galton's initial idea was for a home in the style of a 'comfortable cottage house'. He was presumably influenced by his architect, for the house he ended up building was in the now-fashionable 'Gothic Revival' style, with something of the character of an abbey, ornamented by pinnacles, battlements and buttresses - nothing at all like the simple, classical hall that Repton had proposed. The Hall was not immediately called Warley Abbey, though that was how Hubert referred to it, Once this name stuck, it is easy to understand why people who knew little about architectural history soon imagined the building to be both considerably older than it actually was, and to be connected in some way with Halesowen Abbey. Some took this 'connection' idea to ridiculous extremes, believing there to be a tunnel between the two, never mind that they are 5 kilometres [3 miles] in distance and 90 metres [300 feet] in altitude apart.

To complete his fashionable house, Galton had the brick building clad entirely in Parker's Roman Cement, an innovative, hard wearing but gloomy rendering, and to heighten the effect, he had the render inscribed so that it resembled blocks of stone. Lugar sited the house to one side of where Repton had recommended, and also set it further back into the woodland. This was apparently because Hubert thought there was nothing more unsightly than 'a bald house'. In consequence, many mature trees had to be felled, while others were left standing in front of the abbey, most notably one mature and distinctive beech tree that appears in many early illustrations of the park, and survives to this day. These obstructions would have restricted the extensive views out from the house that Repton had recommended. Since he had died in 1818, and the house was not completed until the year after, it is probably fair to assume that poor Humphry must have been spinning in his grave!

The house apparently had its own water supply, fed from a reservoir near Warley Hall Farm. It also had extensive cellarage, with no fewer than 3 vaulted wine cellars with slate and stone shelves, an ale cellar and a brewhouse; from this it is fair to deduce that Hubert took seriously the role of host and bon-viveur. Across from the house, two stables were built, with stalls for 8 horses, a corn-room, harness room, coach house and a number of bedrooms for the stable-lads. Around the gated yard were found kennels, a privy and a lead-lined water tank. No reference could be found in plans of the abbey to the existence of an icehouse: however, its position was well-known amongst local children during the 1950s, to whom it was known as the 'crypt'. At this time it was not yet completely infilled, [one local resident recalls being thrown into it as a child] which might explain why the archaeological investigation in December 2005 yielded not only a structure of impressive size and construction, but also, amongst the fill material, one of the original supports for the sundial.

When, where and how the abbey was built is well-documented. Less certainty surrounds the landscaping of the park: exactly when this work began, how long it took, how closely [if at all] Repton was involved in the actual works and the extent to which his blueprint was modified by either the client or his contractor remain mysteries. In some ways, this is understandable. A major building project, like Warley Abbey, has a definite timespan. Plans are drawn up, the scheme approved, work begins, the house is completed, and the client moves in: each stage can be fairly accurately recorded. An equivalent landscaping project is more difficult to chronicle accurately, particularly when it involves modifying what is already there, rather than starting from scratch.

Certain of Repton's Red Book proposals were carried out as he intended. Hedges were removed from around the fields across the meadow, to leave isolated standing trees, around which cattle and sheep grazed, in order to maintain continuity between the farm and the parkland. The woodlands and copses on the far side of the meadow opposite the house were sculpted and remodelled; the temple was built, the stream dammed and a pool created to attract wildlife. A sheltered winter garden was also constructed on the south-western side of the house.

However, Repton's dramatic sweeping driveway from the north was not laid out as he intended: with the house set deeper into the woodland than he had suggested, the drama of this approach would in any case have been weakened. Instead, the main driveway to Warley ran in a gentler curve, roughly north to south, between Beech Lanes [Hagley Road West], Lightwoods Hill and Slatch Lane [Abbey Road]. Each of these entrances was guarded by a cottage-style gatehouse or lodge, also designed by Lugar. The stables complex and nursery garden also ended up closer to the main house than Repton would have considered appropriate.

The works were completed around 1819-20, and the Galton family moved in to Warley Abbey, which was to be their home for the next 20 years or so. It would be good to report that this was a happy time for the Galtons, but evidence suggests the contrary. Three of their four children died young, and this prompted the family to leave Warley and to lease out the abbey [as it was then known]. Throughout the remainder of the nineteenth century a succession of families lived there, each one leaving its mark on the building. We know, for example, that the abbey was extended at least once, probably during the 1860s whilst under the care of Sampson Hanbury. An entire new wing was added, in exposed brickwork and to a 'Tudor' style, with a small cupola or bell-tower. This nod to a bygone era was clearly enough, some years later, to convince the authorities that the abbey was a genuine antiquity.

During the 1880s and 1890s the abbey was inhabited by newspaper magnate Sir Hugh Gilzean-Reid and his family. He evidently lived in some style there, seeing himself as 'the squire' and throwing lavish parties - prime minister William Gladstone was amongst those who visited Warley at this time. They, in turn, were succeeded by Hugh's daughter Annie, who was married to noted Smethwick industrialist Harold Tangye. In 1902, towards the end of their time there, the Tangyes supported the Smethwick Poor Children's Fresh Air Fund, by throwing open the grounds of the Abbey to two thousand poor children from Smethwick, who were fed and entertained.

11 Another Lugar drawing, this time of Warley Abbey as it was when first built, around 1820.

12 · 13
Views of Warley Abbey taken c.1905, shortly before the opening of the public park.

14 Timber clearance in the park, prior to opening: February 1905.

15 - 16 - 17 June 9th 1906 – opening day celebrations in Warley Park,

Smethwick Telephone *10th February, 1906*

"They [Smethwick Council] utterly failed to respond to the challenge and thus to strengthen the hands of those who were pleading for Smethwick to take some worthy part in a scheme which had evoked so much admiration and enthusiasm, and which will result in immense benefit to subsequent generations. Through private generosity Smethwick is happily identified with the purchase of Warley Park. In many ways the residents and the manufacturers have aided the funds; and this stands to the credit of the borough, however much the municipality may have failed in attaining the standards of generosity which our neighbours set up."

Birmingham Post *11th June, 1906*

"On Saturday afternoon the Lord Mayor of Birmingham (Coun. A. Reynolds) formally dedicated to the use of the public Warley Woods and Park, an extensive and beautifully-timbered tract of country on the borders of Edgbaston and Smethwick, which, through the energy of Mr. A. Chance, and a number of other public-spirited citizens, has been saved from the despoiling hands of the speculative builder"
"Saturday was a day of the happiest omen for the opening ceremony. The sun shone brightly in an unclouded sky, the fresh green foliage of a thousand tall trees was stirred by a gentle breeze, and looking over the undulating expanse, dotted here and there with groups of happy holiday-makers, it was difficult to believe that a great city could be so near. The attendance was worthy of the occasion. Whilst the speeches were being made a crowd of many thousands pressed around the enclosure, and during the latter part of the afternoon and in the evening a constant stream of visitors strolled through the woods and across the spacious park, admiring the beauty spots which every turn unfolded" ..."The police arrangements for the day were controlled by Supt. Hill (Oldbury) and Insp. Brazier (Hales Owen) who had a staff of forty-eight constables in and around the park."

Birmingham Gazette and Express *11th June, 1906*

"The languishing bluebells in the Warley Woods took their last look at the sun on Saturday. One moment nodding peacefully in a June siesta; the next, gripped relentlessly by grubby hands and borne bodily away by budding citizens. The Warley Woods were thrown open for all time to the public, and the public's children plucked nosegays for souvenirs. Instinct made them as callous as the builder, as determined as the tree feller."

Smethwick Telephone *16th June, 1906*

"One can hardly realise at present the extent to which Bearwood will be affected by the opening of Warley Woods and Park as a "People's Park". The traffic on the trams to Bearwood, both Saturday and Sunday, was enormous, while the Bearwood Road is becoming more popular than "The Mile" as a promenade."

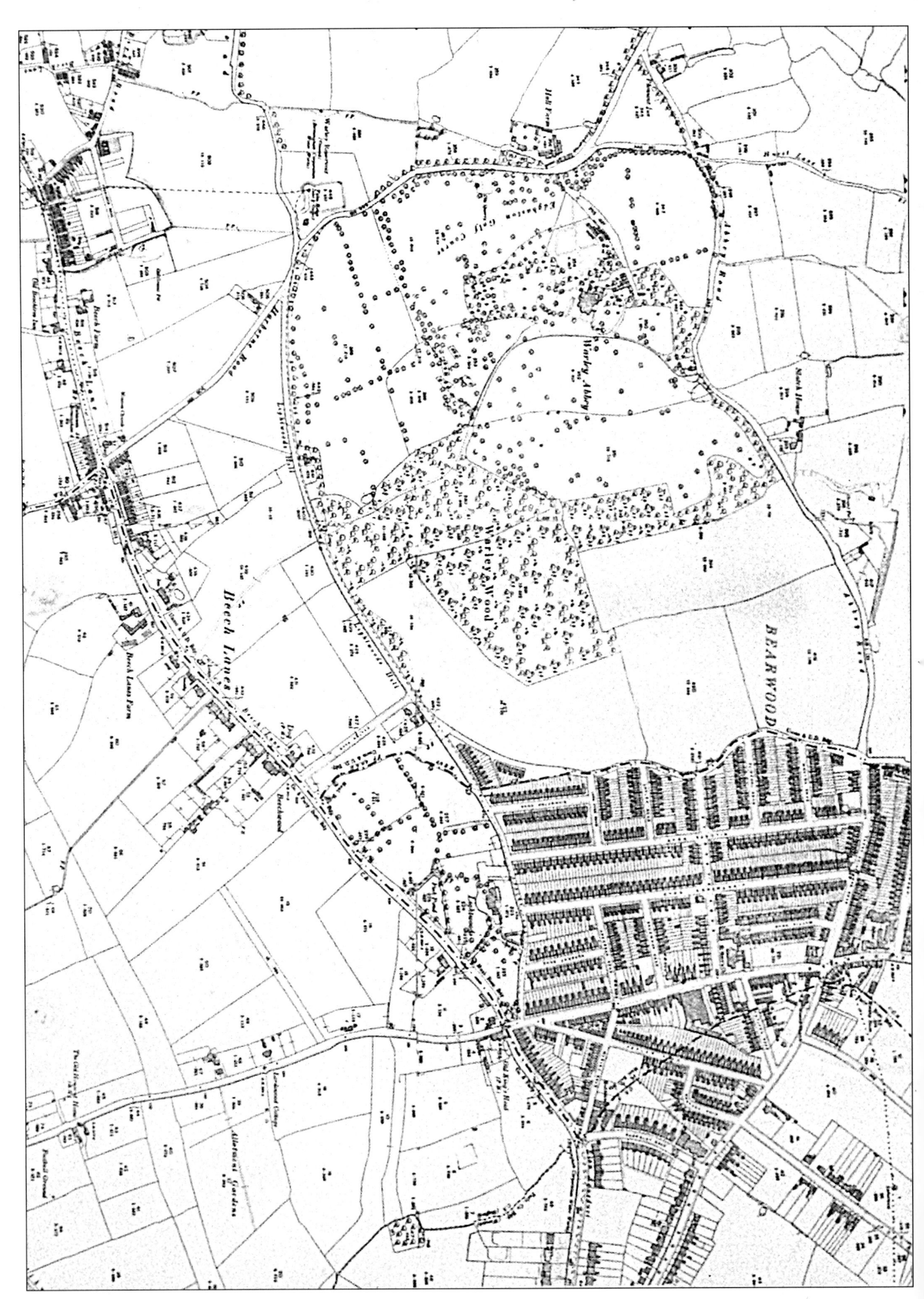

18 This Ordnance Survey plan c.1902 shows Warley Park and Edgbaston Golf Course, before part of the estate was sold for housing and the remainder became the public park.

The Opening of the Public Park

By the turn of the century, the Warley Hall estate had been broken up. In 1902, Tangye sold the house and parkland to William Henry Jones; factory owner, contractor, and owner of a quarry in Abbey Road. It seems fair to assume that Jones, unlike his predecessors, did not buy the estate in order to pursue the life of the country gentleman in Warley Abbey. Jones was a property speculator, whose vision was to develop the site with homes for the aspiring lower middle classes, and secure for himself a decent profit. This process had already begun with the eastern part of the estate, lying between Wigorn Road and Barclay Road. Having passed to two great nephews of Hubert Galton, Captain Leonard and Major Hubert, this land was sold in 1901 for £19,000 to the Freehold Land Building Society, of Birmingham. The entire block of land was then, between 1901 and 1910, sold off in small development plots, cleared of trees and developed with houses 'for the artisan and lower middle classes only'. Strict rules prevented the building of 'back-houses, public houses or manufacturing premises', and ensured this would become, and remain, a 'respectable' suburb.

When Jones tried to do the same with his land in 1905, he met with considerable and possibly unexpected resistance. The importance of the Abbey and its surrounding parkland was beginning to be recognised; today we would use terms like 'green lung' or 'valuable oasis' to describe the park. We would also use the word 'nimbyism' to define the reaction of those who were beginning to purchase or lease houses in Barclay, Galton and Park Roads, attracted there by the parkland right on their doorstep. Now these newcomers, along with other local residents and concerned individuals, discovered there were plans to build houses all over the park they were up in arms. This growing campaign to preserve the unique character of Warley Park was given an impetus, a focus and a voice by the intervention of Alexander Chance, from the world-famous glassmakers, Chance Brothers of Smethwick.

In 1902 he had played a key part in saving nearby Lightwoods Park from development, in very similar circumstances. Now, in 1905, he joined forces with a conservation group, the Selborne Society, to achieve their goal of saving the park from development. They had to raise around £43,000 and required land from several different owners ....and they only had until Easter 1906 to do it.

Contributions from Smethwick and Oldbury Councils, Joseph Chamberlain, Lord Calthorpe and the readers of the Birmingham Evening Mail, combined with the generosity of local residents, saw a total of over £14,500 pledged by January 1906. This was a very impressive figure, but still left the campaign £28,500 short of its target. In a last ditch attempt to save the park, Alexander Chance approached Birmingham City Council for help. He offered them land already secured, money in hand and pledged, together with an option on the remaining land holding, in return for Birmingham making up the difference, and effectively buying and taking over the park. This proposal was a controversial one, particularly since the park lay outside the Birmingham boundary. A Local Government Board of Inquiry was held, early in 1906, to determine the City's application to borrow the £28,500 needed to complete the purchase of the Warley Woods Estate. One of the key arguments in favour of the acquisition was that at that time Birmingham possessed a relatively small acreage of parks and open spaces, relative to its size. The addition of 110 acres, even though sited beyond its boundaries, would enable the council to address this shortfall. It was also stated that Birmingham's intention was to maintain the site in its 'primitive condition' as an open space for public use. The opposing view was made with equal force, namely that the beneficiaries of this scheme would live within Oldbury and Smethwick, and that it was therefore wrong for the ratepayers of Birmingham to meet this expense. Nonetheless, the proposal was eventually approved and on Saturday June 9th 1906 Warley Park was opened by Birmingham's Lord Mayor, Alfred Reynolds.

Thousands of people filled the park for this joyous ceremony, and in his opening speech, Alexander Chance prophetically said-

"I want it to be known as the People's Park, for there never was a park in the Midlands that was paid for directly by the money of the people"

This notion of 'The People's Park' is one that has, since 1996 inspired and guided members of what is now Warley Woods Community Trust, in their quest to halt the decline and secure the restoration of this uniquely special and inspiring place.

During the ceremony, the Lord Mayor was presented with a silver key, richly gilded, with which he unlocked the principal entrance door to Warley Abbey. In his speech he gave strong hints that both Smethwick and Oldbury councils would be approached, with a view to obtaining from each of them an annual contribution towards the upkeep of the place. Local news reports from the time noted that there were many from Smethwick at the opening ceremony, and that **"not a few wished that Smethwick had been identified, as a municipality, with the scheme, which has attained such a happy consummation"**. Fast forward exactly 100 years, to find identical conversations in place between Warley Woods Community Trust and Sandwell Council [successor to both Smethwick and Oldbury], regarding the need for the council to demonstrate a tangible commitment towards the costs of maintaining the park as an amenity for local residents and council tax payers.

Almost two years to the day after this opening ceremony, in 1908, Alexander Chance returned to Warley to formally open the new entrance to the park from Barclay Road, opposite Upper St Mary's Road. Another two years passed, and in 1910 a further celebration took place when the lease that had been granted to Edgbaston Golf Course for 42 acres of the park expired. This land, too, was incorporated into Warley Park, and became known as 'The New Part'. Cliché collectors should note that at this opening ceremony, Birmingham's then-Lord Mayor referred to the enlarged site of Warley Park as **"The Jewel in the Crown of all the city parks"**.

There remained two further challenges. Firstly, the Birmingham Freehold Land Building Society still owned a strip of land along the western side of Barclay Road, at the time used as allotments, but purchased to build a line of houses to match those opposite. Again, Chance masterminded a campaign to thwart these plans, firstly by obtaining a lease on the allotments, and then by forming a committee to raise the £5,500 that was needed to buy the land outright. In 1910, he formed the Warley Woods Self Help Society, and gained support for the cause by painting a stark though humorous image of the view from the park being of **"hundreds of houses with washed clothes dangling on the lines"**.

He set up an appeal fund, this time aimed squarely at the newcomers who had come to live in the 400 or so houses between Wigorn Road and Barclay Road. In the event, donations came in from far and wide, since Warley Woods was then, and still is, a place that touches people's affections. By 1915, the necessary funds had been raised, and a further piece of the park was secure. Two remaining plots of land (believed to be near the corner of Barclay Road and Lightwoods Hill) were added to the park early in 1916. With that, Warley Park as we know it was finally complete, and Alexander Chance, the man who had made it all possible, had achieved his goal. Perhaps his tireless campaigning and fundraising over more than a decade had finally taken its toll, for he died the following year, in 1917.

19 The Warley Woods Self-Help Society was formed in 1910, in order to prevent the further encroachment of housing into what remained of the park.

20 Anyone approaching Warley Woods from Upper St. Mary's Road would have been faced by this view of the entrance to the park, which was added in 1908.

21 · 22 · 23
Three postcards of Warley Park after it had opened to the public.

The *top* and *middle* views both show the meadow, looking north towards Abbey Road: on the first, sheep graze, whilst the second shows people strolling on grass that looks worn and tussocky.

The *lower* card shows the view from the abbey gardens, looking over the railings at the meadow towards Barclay Road, with many more trees than now.

The Heyday of the Public Park: 1906-1939

The opening of the park in 1906 was a cause for celebration, and prompted an era when Warley Woods became an extremely popular destination for people from all across the western side of Birmingham. At weekends and on bank holidays people came in their thousands from Ladywood and Edgbaston, by tram or bus to the Bear or the Kings Head, and then on foot.

The park had been transformed from a private estate into a public park in various subtle ways, but the intrinsic qualities of the landscape remained much the same. The stock control fences were taken down, and additional woodland walks were constructed, with new gravelled paths through the winter garden. The main driveway was planted with non-native, specimen trees, such as blue cedars. A number of new structures were added at key locations around the park, to act as focal points. These included a bandstand, two drinking fountains, wishing well, arbour, several shelters and an aviary. Many of these features were donated by local businessmen, often after a bit of prompting from Chance: the bandstand and chairs, for example, were provided by Smethwick brewer Edward Cheshire. In his opening–day speech, Chance mentioned that he had found a source of good seats at 28s [£1.40] each, and his aim was to get 500 donated through 5 wealthy friends. Exactly how successful he was in this quest remains a mystery, though early postcards of the park do clearly show large numbers of rustic timber seats around the bandstand and abbey. The park was fenced with ornamental railings and gates, and, like all parks then and ever since, there seemed to be notices everywhere, mainly warning visitors of all the things they were not allowed to do in the park! It was to be open the same hours as Birmingham's other parks, i.e. 6am – 9pm (or sunset), and a bell was rung half an hour before closing time.

Despite the restrictions and regulations, this new park must have seemed like paradise for the working people living in the industrial streets of Birmingham. Specimen trees, ornamental shrubs and flower beds, connected by networks of footpaths; ample seats from which to enjoy the views; shelters for when it rained; a bandstand with regular entertainment provided; a pool for children to paddle in; tennis courts and a tearoom in the abbey that could cater for wedding receptions – all these factors contributed to making Warley Woods a park without equal.

Even with these additions, the park retained its qualities of openness and scale, and these were key factors in accounting for its popularity. This was a slice of countryside within the city, an accessible playground for the masses in the days when real countryside was out of reach of ordinary working people. However, there remained a distinct division between the public part of the park, such as the meadow, driveway and arboretum, where free access was allowed, and the private areas – the walled garden and glasshouses, most of the abbey except for the tearoom - that remained off-limits to the masses. In some ways the traditions of the private estate from the 19th century still lived on. Once the bell had rung and the park gates locked, it must have been a quiet, empty and at times spooky place.

In 1910, Oldbury Council built Abbey School in a corner of the park at the junction of Abbey and Barclay Roads. This quickly became a community focus for meetings, lectures, concerts, dances and fundraising events. In 1917 a Sunday School was established there, and this continued to operate until Warley Woods Methodist Church was opened, in 1929. A gate in the corner of the school playground gave access directly into the park, which was used both as a playing field, and for outdoor lessons. Because of the size, openness and bowl shape of the meadow, it became established as a venue for several major events and gatherings – for example, in 1909, the Boy Scouts held a huge open-air meeting and demonstration, attended by their founder Baden Powell, while the same year saw the park host a juvenile rally of the Independent Order of Rechabites.

The period between the opening of the public park in 1906 and the outbreak of the Second World War was probably the heyday of Warley Woods as a pristine and manicured public open space. In many ways this was largely down to the vision, diligence and determination of one man: George Bretherick, Park Superintendent from 1906-1935. He already worked for Birmingham Parks Department and was selected to oversee the development and management of this prestigious new park when it opened in 1906. He and his family therefore moved in to the so-called "new wing" of the abbey - presumably this referred to the 1860s extension.

He had a staff of eighteen gardeners under his control, together with keepers, parks police, even a carter and his shire horse. It is also known that George's first love was horticulture, and the glasshouses within the walled garden were his domain. It was here that he grew flowers and bedding plants for the ornamental flower-beds around the park. His particular passion was roses; in 1911 he set about creating the rose garden, with its grid of paths and sundial, from scratch, and by the 1930's there were reputed to be 150 varieties of rose on display. The nursery also supplied cut flowers for the Council House in Birmingham, and put on magnificent displays of both flowers and vegetables for Birmingham's great horticultural shows. Fruit and vegetables were grown in abundance throughout this period, in the greenhouses and the orchards. Elsewhere within the walled gardens there was a mushroom house, with a series of steaming heaps of compost and leaf litter. The Brethericks also kept cattle, pigs and poultry.

As part of the war effort during the First World War, parts of the park were turned over to food production, particularly vegetables; the strip of land along Barclay Road, for example, having recently been saved from housing development and incorporated into the park, was laid out as allotments. Elsewhere around the site pigs, poultry and sheep were kept. During the period 1914-1916, up to 50

24 Lightwoods House, believed to date from 1791, stands to this day in nearby Lightwoods Park, and was used as a military hospital during the First World War.

Belgian refugees were accommodated in the abbey and the families helped out with food production around the park, under Bretherick's supervision. From 1916 onwards, the refugees left, but Lightwoods House [in Lightwoods Park] became a military hospital. Soldiers convalescing here helped out on the land and, again under George's guidance, were trained for civilian careers in agriculture. Despite these labour windfalls, it was difficult to maintain the park throughout the war years, with menfolk away fighting, and women were drafted in to help out. One of these was Gertrude Rymer, Birmingham Parks Dept's first woman gardener; coincidentally she was the daughter of George Rymer, the head gardener to Sir Hugh Gilzean-Reid, and was brought up in Lightwoods Lodge.

The park and grounds were well looked after, even through the difficult wartime period. The same could not be said of the abbey itself; it was probably somewhat rundown when Birmingham took it over in 1906, having passed through various owners in the years leading up to handover. The Parks Department probably invested more in the infrastructure of the park than in the building itself, and by the end of the First World War its condition had deteriorated to such an extent that it was declared unsafe and there were calls for it to be demolished. This threat was effectively countered when the abbey was scheduled as a building of historic importance, based on the false premise that it really was an ancient abbey ["parts of which date back to the Plantagenets" i.e. the 15th century according to the publication "Birmingham Faces and Places"]. Lugar and Galton's collusion in designing a throwback building a century before had clearly worked. Nonetheless, the continued poor state of the abbey apparently gave rise to further calls for its demolition during the 1930s, despite its "historic" status.

In 1921 the golf course re-opened, and six years later the abbey took on a second lease of life, when it became the clubhouse and golf shop, as well as continuing to serve as a tea-room for the general public. A. J. Padgham was appointed as the resident golf professional to the course, and part of the abbey was converted into a home for him. During the 1930s an additional ground floor room in the abbey was made available as a club-room for the golf club that had now been established at the course. William Powell, who had joined Bretherick in 1916 when he was invalided out of the army, worked in the park and the nursery until he became one of the first groundsmen on the re-opened golf course, a post he held until his retirement in 1956.

Meanwhile, the strip of land on the western side of Barclay Road that had been turned over during the war to allotments, was laid out as tennis courts, between Abbey Road School and the entrance opposite Upper St. Mary's Road, with a bowling green beyond. Both these facilities were served from a thatched hut, which acted as ticket office and changing room; remains of its concrete base can still be seen near where the pathway from Barclay Road enters the meadow at the edge of the tree belt.

However, the period between the two world wars saw the rapid growth and suburbanisation of Birmingham, Smethwick and Oldbury. As new housing estates were built ever nearer to the park, the stage was set for one of the biggest single changes to the setting of Warley Woods; the remodelling of Abbey Road in 1925-27. Until the mid-1920's, Abbey Road as we now know it ended at Barclay Road. Towards Bearwood, there was a tight grid of terraced streets, well-paved and lit, much as now. From Abbey School westwards, however, it continued as little more than a cart track, known as Slatch Lane. It was narrow and winding, and in following the natural contours of the ground, presented very steep slopes that motor vehicles found difficult to negotiate. At a time when land for building was in great demand, the state of this road was a real impediment to further development.

Oldbury Council took the decision to rebuild Slatch Lane, and work began in 1925. The entire length that borders the park, from Barclay Road to Harborne Road, was widened and completely reprofiled. In order to reduce the steepness of the slopes, material was removed from the two high points, and deposited at the low point. This process involved building new retaining walls alongside Abbey School, and opposite what is now Pitcairn Road. The course of the new road was raised across the valley floor, between the north lodge and Alexander Road. This affected the outfall to Repton's pool, in effect damming it, but since the purpose of these improvements was to open up additional land for housebuilding [of which there was an acute shortage in Smethwick at the time] extensive drainage works were also carried out. The course of the occasional stream through the meadow was therefore re-engineered, the pool was partly infilled and an outlet sluice constructed, with the downstream portion behind Alexander Road culverted to reduce the risk of flooding to the new housing. The completion of this work in 1927, together with the transfer in 1928 of over 500 acres of land from Oldbury to Smethwick [after a long and acrimonious dispute between the two councils] together led to an explosion of housebuilding to the north of Abbey Road. In a few short years the setting for the park had been radically and irreversibly changed. The view out from the driveway past the lodge, or across the former pool, was no longer of a country lane with fields, rolling hills and a farmstead beyond; now Warley Park was firmly part of suburbia.

The gradual loss of this sense of rurality, combined with greater personal mobility and increasing car ownership, provided people with wider choice and an ability to travel further distances for recreation. The vast crowds that had been seen before the war no longer came to Warley Woods. The Lickey Hills, which had been donated for public recreation by the Cadbury family in 1905, became Birmingham's playground of choice, particularly after 1924 when the tram line was extended to Rednal, and on bank holidays the trams ran at 30 second intervals to shift the vast crowds.

25 This card shows gateposts, railings and a shrubbery at the entrance to Warley Abbey, all long since gone.

26 The north side of Warley Abbey; the main entrance was up the steps, between the two lamps.

27 The south side of the abbey, shortly after the opening of the park. The entrance to the tearoom was through the doorway on the left.

28 The south side of the abbey again, looking towards the meadow and showing the distinctive tree that still marks this spot. Four ladies with bicycles approach the tearoom in this delightful postcard filled with life and activity, which captures perfectly the elegance of the Edwardian era.

29 A 1920s postcard view of the abbey in its woodland setting.

30 George Bretherick in his head gardener's uniform stands proudly in the abbey garden, in this posed Edwardian view.

31 The message on the back of this card of the abbey garden reads:

"I have been to Warley woods today with children & staff. It has been a lovely day. We all came by tram to Bearwood & had a lovely walk to Woods. They are just now clothed in all their spring beauty. The gardener took us round the private gardens, tennis courts and market nurseries. There were fruit trees in abundance & such fine shows of flowers. The Abbey in the grounds is a beautiful building & is used as refreshment rooms. There are still a great number of rooms not in use. It commenced to rain about 4.30 just as the children were going to have their photos taken."

32 A rare glimpse of the courtyard and stables, showing the stable lads' accommodation.

33 Bretherick and his staff, at work in the woods c.1912.

34 A postcard of the thatched summer arbour: the girl with the modern-looking bicycle and three of the four boys also appear in *view 27*.

35 Repton's Doric temple is depicted here in an Edwardian postcard. However, the view itself is older, since the temple is intact. This may well be the earliest photographic record we have of the park.

36 · 37 These two fascinating images were both taken on the same day in February 1905, and appear to show the temple being dismantled, apparently following terminal damage from a falling tree: note the heap of bricks.

38 The title of this postcard, sent in 1909, was "Ruins of the old temple".

39 There used to be several shelters in the park; this one stood on the south-eastern side of the meadow, in an area now occupied by young trees.

40 · 41 Two views of the covered drinking fountain, the base of which can still be seen in the woodland, near to where the driveway enters the meadow; the notices read *"the public are requested to protect that which is provided for their own enjoyment"* and *"no dogs allowed in this park unless under control with cord strap or chain"*

42 · 43 Contrasting views of the thatched bandstand and its rows of rustic wooden seats.

44 The drinking fountain was to the same design as two in Lightwoods Park: this is the only feature of the park that survives today, if only as a ruin, (see pictures 98, 99, 100).

45 · 46 These 'then and now' views show the branch of the main drive that links to the corner of Barclay Road and Lightwoods Hill. The carriageway surface had all-but vanished in the photo taken in February 2006.

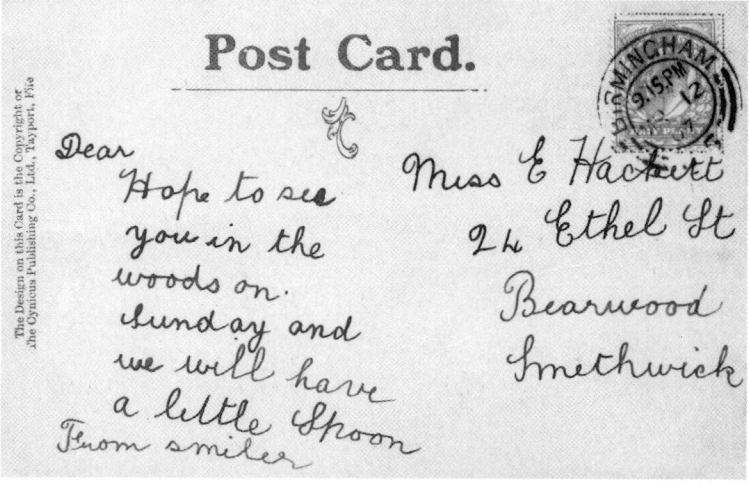

47 · 48 Two sides of the same postcard: it is clear that by 1907 Warley Woods had become well-established as a place for courting couples to meet for 'a little spoon'!

34 WARLEY WOODS, SMETHWICK – CENTENARY OF THE PEOPLE'S PARK

49 This helpfully-dated card shows Baden-Powell (marked with a small white 'x') inspecting a large boy-scouts parade, on July 17th 1909.

50 Another scouts demonstration in Warley Woods the following year.

The Rookery at the French Gardens Warley Woods May 1910

51 · 52 Despite our best efforts, we have so far been unable to discover more about the event shown in these two fascinating postcards, which date from May 1910. They appear to show themed demonstration gardens, put together by seed stockists and nurserymen, presumably to show off their products and landscaping skills. George Bretherick is easy to pick out, and the location appears to be near the current 7th green of the golf course.

French Gardening at Warley Woods, by Sutton and Sons, Reading May 1910

53 The Lodge, Lightwoods Hill showing the entrance to the carriage drive. A plaque on the wall reads "County Police Station," c.1906.

54 A later postcard of the same lodge, sent in 1922. The noticeboard reads "Worcestershire County Council Infant Welfare Centre: attendance Thursdays 2pm – 4pm".

55 Lightwoods Hill looking east in 1927. The chimneys on the left belong to the lodge at the park entrance, Beechwood Road is on the right.

56 The same view in 2006; the lodge is believed to have been demolished in the 1930's.

57 An early view of the Abbey Road lodge, c.1910, clearly showing the gateway and two different styles of railing. Rolling hills and green fields lie beyond the lane.

58 The same scene in 2006; the lodge has gone but the drive survives. Houses beyond were built around the late 1920s, after Abbey Road was improved. The Trust's plans include reinstating the park gates and railings, and resurfacing the driveway.

59 This postcard depicts the lodge in the 1950s. By now the bottom of Abbey Road had been widened and raised; railings and gates were removed as part of the war effort. Note that the driveway appears neatly-edged and newly surfaced. The lodge is believed to have survived into the 1960s.

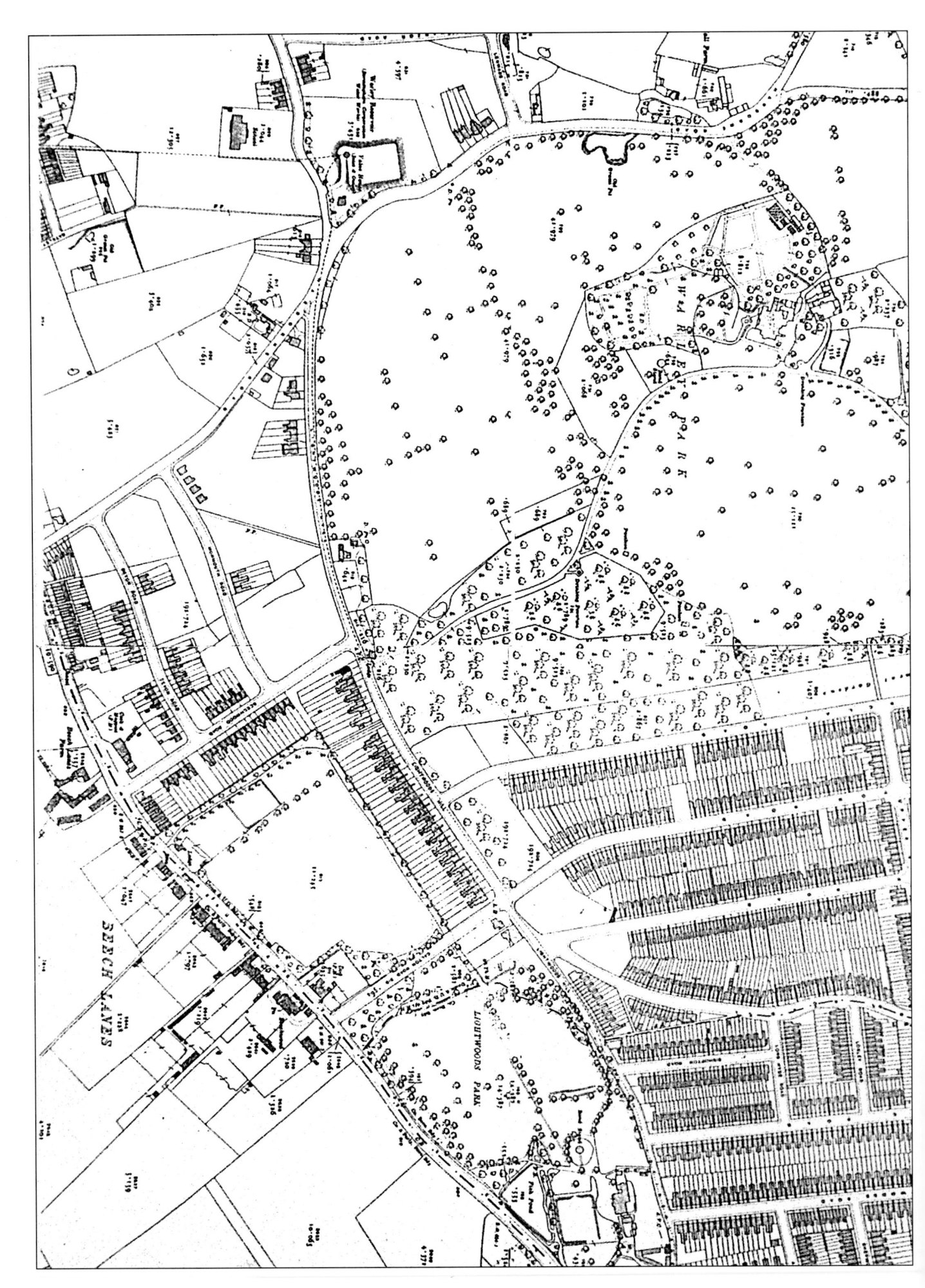

60. Ordnance Survey map of the woods, dated 1913-14, showing the surrounding development. Note the strip of land to the west of Barclay Road marked out for housing plots; even then the woods were not safe from housing development.

61 A charming study of the pool, opposite Abbey Road lodge, taken around 1913 and showing children paddling.

62 Although the pool has been lost as a permanent feature, it still forms after exceptionally heavy rain, as this July 2000 view confirms.

63 The rose garden, in a 1920s postcard: the message reads:
"In the summer this place is covered with rambler roses. You walk under them for quite a distance."

64 A delightful shot of the rose garden, again from the 1920s, featuring two fashionably dressed ladies of the time.

65 · 66 · 67

The sundial formed a simple but attractive centrepiece to the rose garden, as seen in these views from c.1915 [65], c.1938 [66] and the 1950s [67]. One of the sundial's legs was discovered during archaeological survey work in 2005.

THE WINTER GARDEN

SURVEY OF WARLEY ABBEY

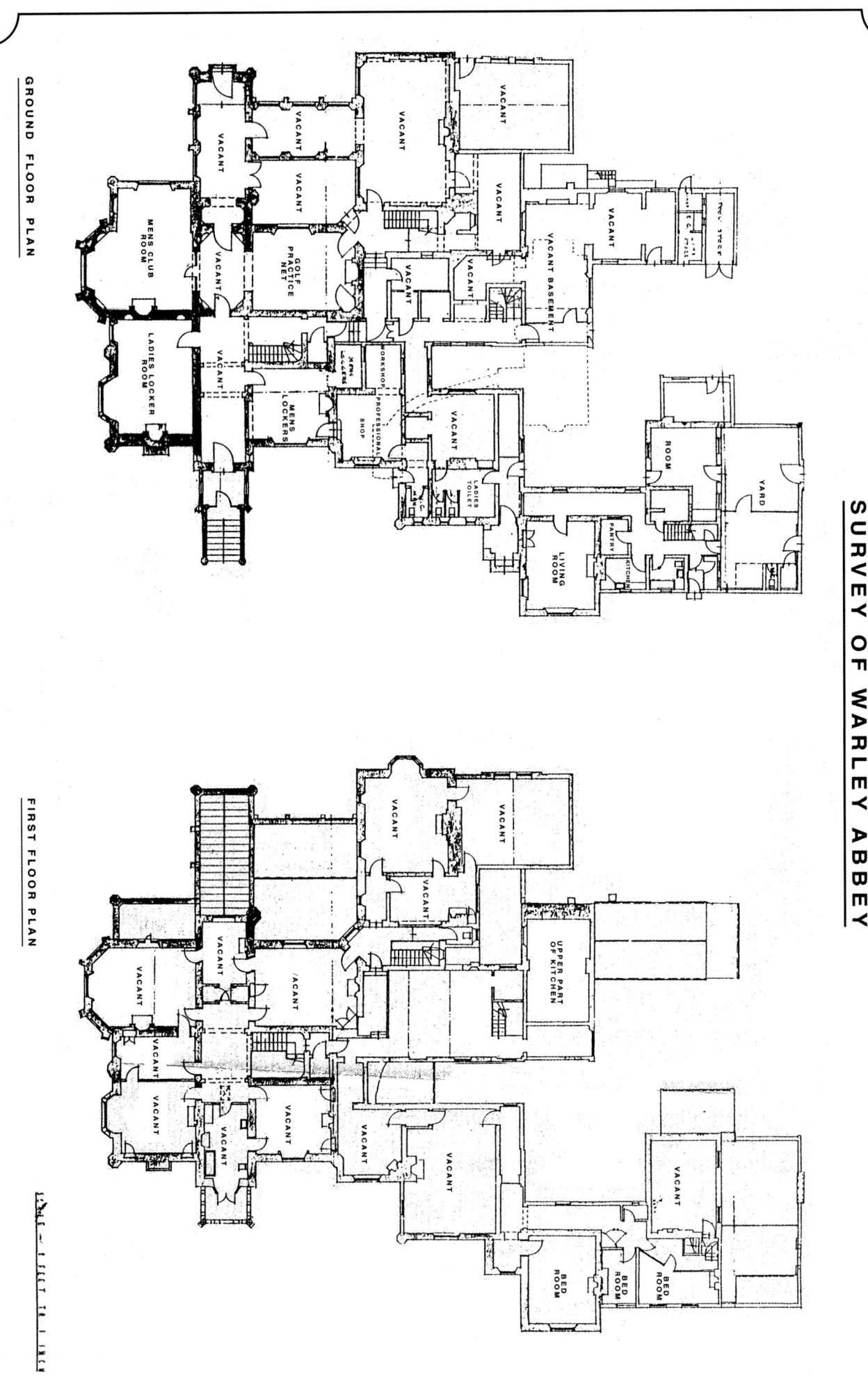

GROUND FLOOR PLAN

FIRST FLOOR PLAN

68 Plan of Warley Abbey c.1950: note how much of the building was vacant when used as the golf clubhouse, but interestingly one room was made into a golf practice net.

History of Warley Woods Golf Course

Warley Woods Golf Course is, at 2673 yards, one of the shorter nine-hole golf courses. However, its hills and slopes more than make up for its lack of length, while its situation within a Repton-designed landscape makes it an unusual, beautiful and inspiring place in which to play. It is one of the oldest municipal courses in the area, and it attracts golfers of all abilities. It is playable by the novice, but remains a challenge for the more experienced golfer.

The course occupies the highest part of Warley Woods, and makes up just over a third of the total site area. On account of its lofty position, and the exposure of some holes to winds from all points of the compass, it is possible to experience several seasons in the same round of golf. If the weather often adds a challenging element to a round of golf at Warley, the underlying geology of the site is beneficial. The bunter pebble and sand that lies beneath the course is exceptionally well-drained, and this factor allows the course to be open for play during even the wettest of spells, when other courses are shut.

Golf is known to have been played on this site since 1896, when Edgbaston Golf Club took out a lease on this land. However, the golf handbook of 1927 named champion golfers who learned at Warley during the 1880's. Much of the golf course formed part of the Warley Hall Estate, which was at that time in the hands of Sir Hugh Gilzean-Reid. Whilst the loss of the parkland must have been something of a blow, the additional rental received from the golf club would have been extremely welcome at this time. We should also remember that very little of the golf course would actually have been visible from the Warley Abbey by then, particularly after Repton's landscaping had been in place for about 75 years, and would have formed mature screens and canopies to hide unwanted views.

The course was laid out so that holes 1,2,7,8 and 9 occupy land that previously belonged to Lightwoods Farm, whilst holes 3,4,5 and 6 were on land that formed part of the Warley Hall estate, and cross Repton-designed parkland. We assume that the changing and mess facilities stood where the existing golf compound stands today. This could have originally formed part of the farm buildings to Lightwoods Farm, and it may be that certain of the existing buildings were adapted to a new use. There is no evidence that there was a clubhouse, as such.

Golf was clearly different in those far-off days, as a case brought before the High Court in 1899, between Edgbaston Golf Club and its landlord, Mr Summerton of Lightwoods Farm, illustrates. The golf club paid £45 a year rental, and had the right to do everything necessary to turn the land into a golf course, while the landlord was to graze sheep and cattle to keep the grass down. In the event, he grazed horses as well, which, by virtue of being shod, damaged the greens. The landowner countered this claim by stating that golfers drove the sheep, causing some to lose their lambs, and that, by cutting the grass, the Club caused suffering to the animals by depriving them of food. Neither side obtained an outright win in the courts, and the solution seemed to include 'fencing the greens'.

When Alexander Chance stepped in to help save the park from being developed for housing in 1906, the lease on the golf course still had four years to run. However, it was clearly his intention that this use would cease, and that this part of the site would eventually be included within an enlarged area of public parkland and open space. This took place in 1910 to much celebration, and contemporary views show sheep grazing over the former golf course. Meanwhile, Edgbaston Golf Course had moved to Ridgacre Road in Quinton.

It is reasonable to speculate that when Birmingham City Council took over responsibility for the now lapsed golf course in 1910, the intention was to re-introduce this activity at some point in the future. Golf was a developing sport, popular amongst the lower middle classes who were coming to live in Warley. As well as meeting this local demand, it is also fair to assume that a municipal golf course in this location would be seen as a money-making venture for the council. Any income that could be offset against the considerable expense associated with the upkeep of the abbey and Warley Park would be most welcome. However, Chance was evidently wise to these plans and fought doggedly against them. He mounted a tireless campaign through the pages of the local press, in which he questioned the 'legality, expediency and legitimacy' of the Council's proposals. Birmingham quietly shelved their plans, at least until after Chance had died [1917] and the war had ended.

Soon, the plans for a golf course were dusted off, but local residents took up Chance's campaign, and vigorously opposed these proposals. They demanded that 'the New Part', as it was known, should be retained as open space, for the enjoyment of the majority, and not for the pursuit of a minority sport. There are reports of protests, with banners and placards. There are even tales that as fast as Birmingham erected fences to enclose the new golf course, the protestors tore them down, overnight. Nonetheless, the course reopened for public use in 1921, as a nine-hole pay and play course. From the outset it was popular, and by 1924 it was described as seriously overcrowded. Warley Woods has been operated continuously ever since, making it one of the longest established golf courses in the area. It is unclear to us whether the course was closed during World War 2; there are accounts that parts of the course were ploughed up and planted with wheat, a crop for which the thin, dry, pebbly soil would have been ill-suited.

The first publication of the **Birmingham Municipal Golf Links – Warley Park – Golfer's Handbook** was published for the year 1927-1928, the same year, incidentally, that Warley completed the double by winning both the men's and ladies' team events in the inaugural Birmingham Gazette Trophy [known as the "Blue Riband" of municipal golf championships]. The handbook contains an informative description of the course and its characteristics at the time.

> "Warley Municipal Course belonged originally to the Edgbaston Golf Club and was acquired by the Corporation [Birmingham] in 1906. After certain improvements to the greens and length of holes it was opened as a public course in May 1921.
>
> The course is approximately 41 acres in area, and is enclosed on two sides by stretches of picturesque woodland. It is a sporting course with many natural hazards and affords a fine golfing training. There is a park-like character about the course, which gives it a note of distinction.
>
> A characteristic of the fairways, which are fairly wide and long, is the fine old turf. The putting greens are large and undulating, and in most instances well fortified by ditches and raised bunkers.
>
> David Brown, who in 1886 won the English Open Championship, received his early training on these links, and Jack Burns, who won the Championship at St. Andrew's in 1888, was also at one time at this course.
>
> The 1st hole, a bogey 5, has a length of 332 yds. And two wooden club shots are necessary to

reach the green, which is well bunkered. The 2nd hole, 200 yds long, and a bogey 3, calls for care, as there are artificial hazards to catch a pull or slice, while No. 3, 237 yds long, at which a good player may hole out in four, has an island green which necessitates a well-judged pitch, as there is a gorge on the left. The 4th hole of 220 yards may be done in three, and the 5th, of 245 yards, in four. The 5th green is situate on rising ground and well protected with bunkers. The 6th hole, 415 yards long and a bogey 5, has a remarkably fine fairway, but it is only a scratch man who can reach the green in two, and even then the brassie shot must be straight, or the player will experience difficulty and the entrance to the green is well protected and there is a surrounding sunken bunker. There is a fine woodland view at the 7th which is a rather difficult bogey 4 hole, 346 yards long. The 8th hole, which is 323 yards long, and a bogey 5, is slightly dog-leg with a carry of 140 yards, and to avoid a difficult ridge, the ladies' tee is placed well forward. A pitch shot is required to reach the green. A good player should hole the 9th in four, which is 250 yards long, but careful play is essential, as a number of trees have to be negotiated and the green is tricky.

A golf house adjoins the course with professional's workshop, lockers, etc. Refreshments can be obtained at the bungalow near the golf house or at Warley Abbey, a few minutes walk from the course."

The map of the course shows the layout of the holes, and the facilities mentioned in the last paragraph above are accessed off Lightwoods Hill. The "golf house" was presumably somewhere near, or formed part of, the current groundsmen's compound. Could it be that the "bungalow" referred to here was in fact the Lightwoods Hill lodge to Warley Abbey in yet another role?

In 1928 the course was lengthened from 2568 yards to 2635 yards and in 1933 was again lengthened to 2696 yards (just 23 yards more than the present length). The 1929 handbook showed that hole No 6 had now become hole No 1, and that facilities had moved, probably around 1927.

"The golf house and professionals workshop, office, etc., and refreshment rooms are situate in Warley Abbey, which also adjoins the course."

In 1934 the starting hole was moved back by one to the original (and present) 5th. The course remained in this configuration until the Abbey was demolished and the present clubhouse built in 1957, the layout reverting to the original order.

The abbey was adapted to offer locker rooms, a professional's shop and living accommodation for the professional and his family. In the 1930s, following the establishment of Warley Golf Club, based at the course, an additional room in the abbey was set aside as a clubroom. The course's first professional was A. J. Padgham, whose son Alf Padgham was British Open champion in 1936. It is said that he was the first British golfer to earn a four figure sum from winning a golf tournament [£1000 in the News of the World Championship, held in South Africa]. Warley Woods' other famous son is Kevin Dickens, who joined the club as a junior in the 1970s, going on to play in the European Tour in 1989, in which year he was second in the Belgium Open. In 1998 he represented Britain in the PGA cup against the USA, and Kevin is currently associated with the club as a teaching professional.

As we have outlined elsewhere, the continuing deterioration of the Abbey, and the absence of funds available for its repair, led to Birmingham taking the decision in 1957 to demolish the building. Before this could happen, a replacement clubhouse, changing room and professionals shop had to

Warley Municipal Links

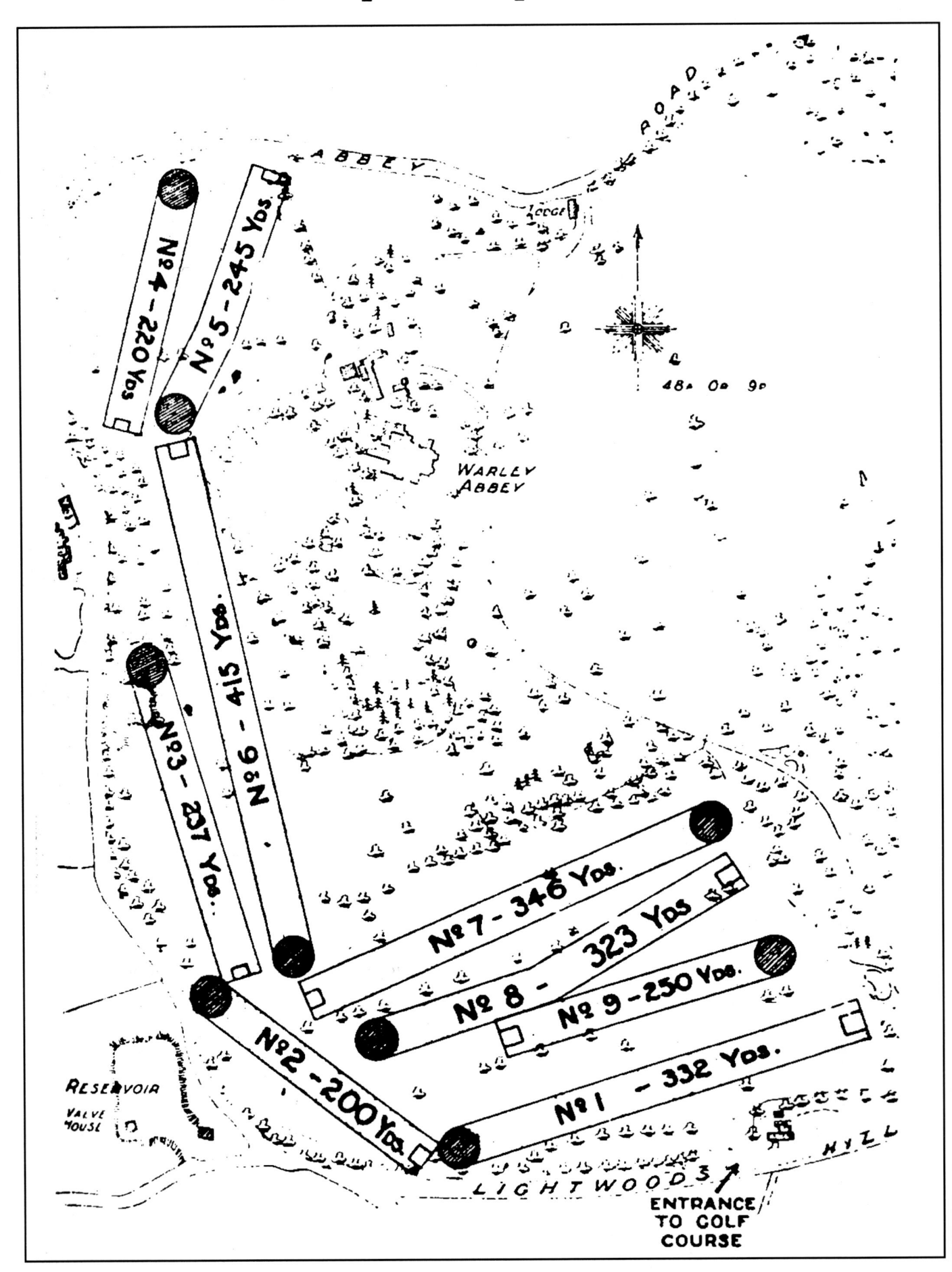

69 This plan of Warley Woods Golf Course appeared in the mid-1920s: it shows the course as recently laid out by Birmingham City Council. Note how it was called Warley Municipal Links, a term nowadays reserved for seaside courses. From 1934 it became Warley Municipal Golf Course.

be built, together with accommodation for on-site staff who were living in the Abbey. A site near the groundsmen's compound, off Lightwoods Hill, was selected, and the existing entrance extended to form a driveway and car park, with a lightweight timber clad structure put up to provide the golf course with the necessary facilities. A pair of semi-detached houses was built, just inside the park boundary but fronting directly onto Lightwoods Hill, to accommodate the head greenkeeper [Bill Mason] and the park superintendent [Frederick Rymer]. Rubble and hardcore from the demolished abbey were used to build up tees and extend the golf course at this time.

Management of the course passed to the Trust in April 2004, and great efforts are being made to improve its attractiveness and 'playability', so as to retain existing customers, and attract new ones, particularly at quieter times. The golf course is one of the Trust's key assets and long term maintenance plans for the whole site will benefit from the income derived from the golf course.

70 Between 1927 and 1957 the Abbey was used as the golf clubhouse. The present golf pavilion, photographed here in May 2006, will be 50 years old in 2007.

71 · 72 Contrasting summer and winter views of the entrance to the golf course, captured in 1981/82 by renowned Smethwick photographer Joe Russell.

73 This picture entitled "Driving from the first tee", appeared in each edition of the golf handbook from 1927 to 1935: the caption changed from 1929 when the first hole became the 5th, and again in 1934 when it became the 6th.

74 The same view in March 2006. Golfers will notice subtle changes: the pronounced ridge has gone and the trees on the right now separate the 1st from the 9th fairway; they also provide a refuge for a sliced ball which rolls off the fairway, leaving a difficult second shot past the oak tree.

75 Another view across the 1st fairway, taken in 1966. The whole course was more open than it is now, but the water tower provides a familiar landmark, although without the mobile phone masts that now decorate it.

76 Another picture from the 1920s, captioned "Pit and Green No.3". Old maps show a quarry at this point, which was presumably adapted into a unique hazard for golfers.

77 The 3rd green in 2006: the 'pit' has gone although golfers still face a steep slope for any ball that goes off to the left of the hole. The tree on the mound may indicate a lowered ground level, which could be the reason why recent archaeological excavations failed to find any trace of Warley Tor, which is believed to have stood nearby.

78 The 7th green in the 1920s. It is possible that this is the location of the pictures of the garden exhibitions in 1910 (51 & 52). If so, this part of the golf course must have been re-made after Edgbaston Golf Club moved out in 1910

79 The 7th green in 2006: the telegraph poles have gone and trees have been planted to separate the holes.

A. J. PADGHAM,
WARLEY PARK MUNICIPAL GOLF COURSE.

CLUB MAKER & COACH.

All Clubs Made Personally, from Wood Specially Selected.

☞ TUITION A SPECIALITY ☜

Every Description of Golfing Requisite in Stock.

80 An advertising page from the 1928 handbook showing the golf professional A.J.Padgham at work in his workshop; this is around the time of his move to the Abbey, and we are unable to accurately place this photograph.

Scale of Charges.

SEASON TICKETS, available for One Year from date of issue:—

Ratepayers or residents within the area of the City of Birmingham .. £3 3 0

Non-ratepayers or persons not resident within the area of the City of Birmingham £5 5 0

Available for all Municipal Courses, extra charge £1 1 0

Available from 1st October to the 31st March—Half the above rates.

Season Tickets can be obtained from the Golf Professional at the Links.

Other Charges.
Payable at the Links.

1/- per round of course (9 holes).

1/**6** for two rounds of course.

Daily Tickets, **2**/-. (Saturdays and Bank Holidays excepted).

Tuition from Golf Professional, **2**/- per hour, plus the charge for an ordinary round of the course; holders of season tickets will not be charged for use of course.

Scoring Cards, **1** d. each. Plan of Course, **1** d.

The Golf Course is open each day as follows:—
WEEK DAYS:
During the Summer, from 7 a.m. to 9 p.m.
During the Winter, from 9 a.m. to Dusk.
SUNDAYS:
During the Summer, from 9 a.m. to 9 p.m.
During the Winter, from 9 a.m. to Dusk.

5

81 Scale of charges from the 1930s. Note that Birmingham residents enjoyed a substantially lower fee, even though the course was then in the borough of Smethwick.

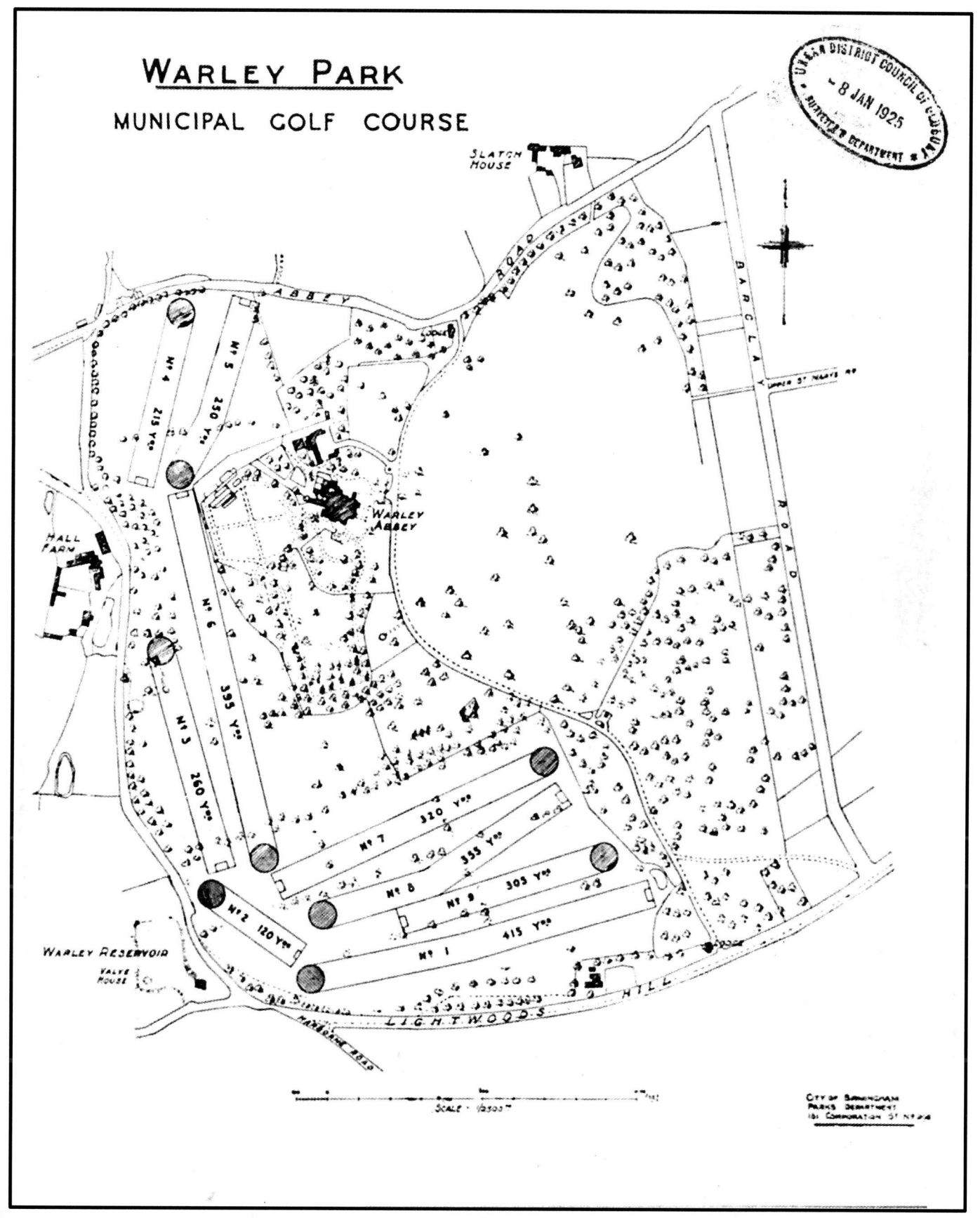

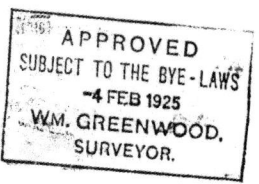

82 This plan of the course from 1925 is stamped by Oldbury council, which suggests that it was related to an application for development.

83 This is believed to be a picture of the golf professional A. J. Padgham, who lived in the Abbey. He is with his son Alf Padgham who in 1936 won the Open Championship.

84 In 1905, a pool was located where the back tee for the 1st hole now stands.

85 Accurately dated to May 1954, this photograph shows the interior of the former abbey drawing room, by now in use as a golf clubroom.

86 These sheep were grazing in the 'new part' in 1913: this was the name given to the land taken into the park from Edgbaston Golf club in 1910. Sheep had been used to keep the grass down on the golf course, although in 1899 the Club had taken their landlord to court when he grazed horses and cattle, as well as the sheep agreed to in the lease.

Warley Woods in World War 2

Smethwick was a highly important industrial centre, with a great number of metal and chemical-based industries, and during World War 2 it became a hive of frenzied activity, with most local companies working flat out to contribute to the war effort. With all these key industries, and because of its closeness to Birmingham, Smethwick also became a prime target for enemy action, and between 1940 and 1942 the town was subjected to ten different air raids by the Luftwaffe.

Although people living close to Warley Woods through this difficult time came to value its peace and tranquillity all the more, the park itself did not entirely escape the effects of hostilities, and suffered several different bombing episodes. The strategic importance of Warley water tower, which had been completed not long before the outbreak of the war, made the park a specific target for bombing action. In December 1940, a parachute mine exploded in the park, close to the water tower. The intention with these devices was that parachutes would slow down the bomb's descent, so preventing it from penetrating the ground where its explosive power would be absorbed, and concentrating the explosive power at ground level where the blast could detonate outwards, to maximum destructive effect. And so it was, for this one explosion apparently caused extensive damage to hundreds of nearby houses, as well blowing the doors and windows out at the water tower itself. The Nazi propagandist Lord Haw-Haw claimed that the tower had taken a direct hit, and been completely destroyed.

In April 1941, it is reported that 200 incendiary bombs fell in a wide swathe from Hagley Road West to the edge of Warley Woods, causing extensive damage across a wide area. A further raid on Smethwick took place in July 1942, where a large bomb fell directly into the woods, uprooting a large tree. Exactly where this bomb fell, within the park, remains a matter of dispute. The Midland Red bus garage on Bearwood Road was also thought to be a likely bombing target, and buses were parked overnight along the main driveway and around the edge of the park, where the risk of attack was reduced.

As well as being a site of enemy action, Warley Woods itself also underwent many changes during the Second World War, as the abbey, grounds and park were adapted to help in the war effort. Part of the abbey was put to use as an Air Raid Precautions [ARP] lookout post, and a base where local people could take their gas masks to have the filters replaced. There was a second ARP command post at the corner of Lightwoods Hill and Barclay Road. The abbey was also used as a base for the Home Guard, whose training exercises in the woods were sometimes incorporated into local children's play activities! Activities of a different kind resulted from the arrival of a large contingent of US servicemen in the area, who were stationed in a camp in Beakes Road, on the site of Mill Garden flats. By all accounts, the GIs became a magnet for local girls and the Woods, in turn, became a magnet for both.

As a back up for fighting fires caused by air raids, the Fire Service established a network of static water tanks at key locations around the area, One stood near the Abbey Road entrance to the park, and another along Barclay Road, near Upper St Mary's Road. These were large circular metal tanks, about 1.8 metres [6ft] tall. The tennis courts along Barclay Road were also dug up, lined with clay and filled with water. A number of surface air raid shelters were built at various points around the park; Harborne Road, Lightwoods Hill – in what is now the golf compound - and one particularly large shelter close to the water tank on Barclay Road. This was apparently also used as a dry store for newspaper salvage, again as part of the war effort. Also in Barclay Road, close to the school stood two pig bins, where local householders would deposit waste food that could be collected and boiled up as pigswill.

Another important campaign during the war was intended to soften the impact of food rationing, and this saw householders encouraged to grow their own food, under the 'Dig for Victory' slogan. Areas of land were allocated and laid out as allotments, and this practice was widespread within Warley Woods. The tennis courts along Barclay Road, between Upper St Mary's Road and the school were converted to allotments, and large parts of the meadow, both sides of the stream, were also turned over to cultivation. Initially potatoes were grown, but many of those grown were dug up and spirited away by local residents. There was also an attempt to grow wheat and other cereal crops, both here and on parts of the golf course even though the thin, dry, stony soil was ill-suited to this purpose. However, this practice continued into the immediate post-war period, such were the pressures caused by acute food shortages. The end of the war was celebrated by Mr Swan, proprietor of the corner shop at the top of Upper St. Mary's Road, re-starting ice-cream production - a popular move, locally.

It is widely known that many of the park railings were removed at this time, and melted down to provide the raw materials to build Spitfires. It is less well-known that much of the metal collected in this way ended up going for scrap, as it was totally unsuitable for the intended purpose. It is also often forgotten that after the war ended, very few of these railings were replaced. Timber paling fences were installed around much of the golf course, and a significant proportion of the Trust's Lottery grant will go towards installing steel railings and gateways, as a replacement for those that were so fruitlessly removed sixty-five years ago.

87 Members of the Home Guard in front of the Abbey during World War Two.

88 Older readers may remember the severe winter of 1947. This photo was taken in February that year, from Harborne Road / Pottery Road, and provides a glimpse of one of the air raid shelters that was still in place at that time, half buried in a snowdrift. We have so far been unable to locate any pictures of the prefabs that stood just along from here, towards Abbey Road.

89 "Warley, showing the junction of Wolverhampton Road and Hagley Road West and the Odeon cinema". Dated to 1950, this aerial shot of a well-known local landmark clearly shows a corner of Warley Woods in the background.

Warley Woods 1945-96
Final flowering and gradual decline

Compared to previous phases in the park's evolution, the latter half of the twentieth century has yielded surprisingly little factual or photographic evidence about what was happening to Warley Woods. The only event that was accurately and carefully chronicled was the demolition of the abbey in 1957.

What we can safely assume is that both the park and the abbey entered the post war era in pretty bad shape. Parts of the park had been turned over during the war to allotments for food production, beauty having taken second place to survival in such difficult times. As in the Great War a quarter of a century earlier, the absence of labour would have stretched the Council's ability to manage and maintain the site to the same high standards that had applied in peacetime. We also know that there had been some bomb damage to part of the park. To meet the housing shortage in the immediate postwar years, a small area of land fronting Harborne Road, between Abbey Road and Pottery Road, was developed with 12 single storey prefabs. These were intended only to have a short life, but were not demolished until the 1960's, when the land reverted to parkland once again.

However, Bimingham clearly retained a strong commitment towards the park, and it continued to thrive under the stewardship of Frederick Rymer, who was descended from a family of gardeners with strong family connections to Warley. He was the park superintendent during the 1950's, with responsibility for the greenhouses, meadow and woods – but not the golf course. He clearly maintained the high standards set a generation earlier by George Bretherick, as contemporary views show the site well-managed and tidy into the early 1960s. At that time the nursery and glasshouse were still producing chrysanthemums for Birmingham's parks displays, while the site continued to act as a tree nursery, again supplying other parks. During the 1950's, Rymer could still muster between fifteen and eighteen staff to work in the park, divided into inside i.e. nursery and greenhouses, and outside gangs, who looked after the remainder of the park.

However, it is fair to assume that the abbey itself, having been in a poor state of repair before war broke out, had to be in a fairly distressed condition by the time it ended, despite having been pressed into service as an ARP control centre and, later, as a welfare centre. Faced with mounting repair bills for the building – a figure of £18,000 was quoted – and no viable long-term use for the majority of the building, Birmingham [after prolonged consideration] took the decision in the mid-1950s to demolish the abbey.

This turned out to be quite a slow and laborious process. Firstly the council had to provide alternative living accommodation for the golf professional and the park superintendent who still lived there. For this purpose, two semi-detached houses were built, fronting onto Lightwoods Hill, immediately alongside the groundsmen's compound. A new golf clubhouse, locker room and professional's shop was also needed, and this took the form of a lightweight, timber-clad pavilion, which arrived on the back of a lorry and was installed behind the new houses. This was presumably intended to be no more than a temporary solution, and we do not know what the long-term intentions of the council were at this time. Interestingly, this temporary building, completed in 1957, remains in use, one year short of its half century.

The abbey was still scheduled as a building of historic importance [despite, presumably, new evidence to the contrary], and the council had to obtain permission from the Office of Works before demolition could proceed. The actual job of demolishing the abbey took place over the second half of 1957. To many local people, this probably seemed both sacrilege, and an isolated act of destruction. The truth is rather different. We know from previous attempts to have the building cleared that it had been in a poor condition for some time, and was living on borrowed time. Photographs taken immediately before its final demise show the full extent of its dilapidation. Personal accounts also refer to the rotten nature of the floor in the clubroom at the time. In many ways, without a long-term viable use for the whole building, its clearance could almost be considered something of a mercy killing. Compare the fate of Warley Abbey with that of Great Barr Hall, the Galtons' previous home. This grand mansion, rebuilt in the 1850s in a Gothic style very similar to Warley, and occupying a magnificent landscaped setting, has simply died of neglect – whether deliberate or accidental – and today presents a desperately sad sight. Furthermore, the demolition of Warley Abbey was part of a far wider process that was taking place all over the country, and research undertaken by the pressure group SAVE, in 2006, estimated that approximately 1600 country houses had been demolished over the past hundred years. A news article from 1957 states:

> **"Soon Warley Abbey will be no more than a memory, but the broad acres of Warley Park will remain for the use and enjoyment of the people of the surrounding district for ever"**

It is easy to pinpoint the reasons why the park subsequently slipped into decline. Steadily reducing budgets for grounds maintenance over many decades have been largely responsible, and the introduction of compulsory competitive tendering in the 1980s made things worse. The understandable response of councils to these financial pressures was to centralise grounds maintenance operations, which resulted in the loss of dedicated, skilled, on-site staff. The absence of a permanent human presence makes it more likely for vandalism and other forms of anti-social behaviour to occur, and for the resulting damage to go unseen, unreported, and unfixed. This in turn sets up a vicious spiral, where the park appears uncared for, the condition of the facilities continues to decline, and use of the park falls.

Warley Woods can be said to have fallen into this unhappy spiral over the past thirty years or so. Almost all the remaining built form structures and features have either been demolished [stables, lodges, glasshouses for example] or gradually fallen into disrepair, like the drinking fountain and the timber fencing around the golf course. A news story from as long ago as 1957 describes the activities of a gang of local teddy boys, one of whom was in court charged with deliberately setting fire to, and destroying, one of the shelters in the park, for which act he was fined £10 with 7s 6d [37 1/2p] costs. Many of the original drives and pathways have become eroded or overgrown, while elsewhere, a new network of informal pathways have become established, to reflect visitors' desire lines into the park from nearby streets. Invasive plant species such as laurel and holly have flourished unchecked, and have created management problems by forming dense barriers, clumps and thickets, that have encouraged den building and anti-social behaviour. Natural processes of decay have been compounded by deliberate acts of vandalism, such as fire-setting and dumping stolen cars.

There are those who place the blame for this firmly with Birmingham City Council, believing that because the park was outside the city's boundaries, it was given a lower priority in resource allocation. This theory is disproved by the reality that this is not a local problem, as evidenced by urban parks the length of the country that have been stripped of resources for their upkeep in exactly the same way as Warley Woods has.

Where Birmingham cannot escape blame, however, is for the systematic and wilful destruction of the glasshouses in 1996. This was seen by many local people as a more blatant act of civic vandalism than the demolition of the abbey forty years before. It was this action that set the scene for the final chapter in our story, the formation of Warley Woods Community Trust.

90 The glasshouses were in full use, and appeared well-maintained, in this photograph from 1952.

91 An unusual view of the Abbey, taken across the meadow with a long lens: June 1950.

92 · 93 By 1956 the Abbey was in a state of terminal decline – note the broken windows and rendering falling away to expose brickwork behind. The golf club was its sole occupier, awaiting the construction of the new golf pavilion, off Lightwoods Hill.

94 · 95 The demolition of the Abbey in 1957 was captured by local photographers, including Joe Russell: note the unsecured demolition site, and the couple on the bench, seemingly unaware of the destruction around them.

96 The strip of land along the western side of Barclay Road might have had houses built, but for the efforts of local people. The portion from the school to about halfway along Barclay Road, once free from the threat of development, was used as tennis courts and a bowling green, and as allotments during the war. In the mid-1950s small trees were planted to extend the woodland right up to Barclay Road. In the background is Mr Swan's sweetshop, a popular place for children, particularly after the removal of sweet rationing in 1953.

97 The same view in 2006: the trees have grown but the sweetshop has closed.

98 Dating from the late 1960s, this is the most recent postcard we have found of Warley Woods. The fountain's roof is still intact, and the flowerbeds appear well-maintained.

99 By 1985 the roof has gone....

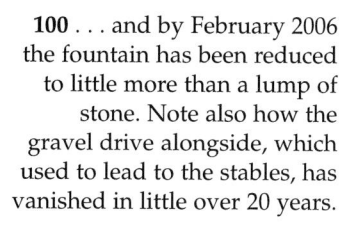

100 . . . and by February 2006 the fountain has been reduced to little more than a lump of stone. Note also how the gravel drive alongside, which used to lead to the stables, has vanished in little over 20 years.

101 A cyclo-cross event in the park, alongside Abbey Road, in 1963.

102 Boys Brigade companies from across Birmingham and Smethwick use Warley Woods for their annual cross-country races. This was the Junior race in October 1993.

103 Smethwick Local History Society has established a tradition of holding an annual picnic evening each summer. This photo from July 1999 shows a group of members, including local historian David Yates, sitting on the log.

Warley Woods Community Trust
1996-2006

The loss of the greenhouses in 1996, and the manner in which these "heritage assets" were destroyed, opened the local community's eyes to the way in which Warley Woods was being managed, and to the state their park was in.

It was around this time that the Heritage Lottery Fund established its Urban Parks Programme, aimed at directing a proportion of the proceeds from the National Lottery to preserve, enhance and widen access to, and enjoyment of, parks, gardens and other urban spaces.

In 1996, an inaugural meeting of local residents was called by local councillor Steve Eling. It was quickly realised that, through its Listed Park status and its Repton connections, Warley Woods should be a prime candidate for Lottery assistance. Officers from Sandwell Council provided tireless and invaluable help with researching, developing and submitting a bid, which took the form of a replica of Repton's Red Book of 1795. After a lengthy wait, 1999 brought the welcome announcement that £1 million had been approved for the restoration of the park. The work was to include woodland management, new perimeter railings around the golf course and parts of the park, gateways and entrances, reconstruction of the main driveway and other paths, new benches and archaeological survey work.

In November 1999, at a meeting at Abbey School attended by 130 people, Warley Woods Community Trust was established, with Steve Eling as chair. In many ways this initiative mirrored the establishment of Chance's Warley Woods Self-help Society, almost a century before. Although the grant was made to the Trust, the restoration process is to be managed jointly by WWCT and Sandwell MBC, with the freehold of the land remaining with Birmingham City Council. The process of drawing up a lease on the site, for 99 years, between Birmingham and Sandwell, and between Sandwell and the Trust, took nearly three years to complete. In 2002, the whole site, including the golf course, passed out of Birmingham's control, initially to Sandwell, and finally in April 2004 to the Trust.

In 2002, the Trust was successful in obtaining a further substantial grant, this time from the Big Lottery Fund, to restore the winter garden and arboretum areas, which fell outside the scope of the original approval. This work, which includes the construction of new accessible paths and woodland walks, landscape management, sculptural features and a woodland play area, started during 2006, following consultation at the Picnic in 2005, and with local schoolchildren in 2006.

Despite some delays and setbacks, the Trust has made noticeable progress since taking over the site in 2004. After many years of neglect and decline, the backlog of work is being tackled. This has involved both Trust staff and many local volunteers. Together, they have pruned back shrubs, lifted and thinned thickets, taken down overhanging branches, removed invasive plants, cleared and resurfaced some well-used paths, and undertaken regular litter-picks. Volunteers have also been responsible for transforming the café and professional's shop in the golf pavilion, and for building from scratch an office for the Trust. The willingness shown by so many people to get involved with the Trust is one of its key strengths.

Since 2002 the Trust has hosted a Picnic in the Park every July, with free, live music, entertainment and activities, attracting large crowds of local people. The 2006 Centenary Picnic is being planned as this book goes to press, and we hope that this special event will capture something of the spirit of the 1906 opening ceremony.

In December 2005 a professional archaeological investigation took place, involving a series of trial trenches dug at sites of known features around the park. The findings were reported in March 2006 and are both encouraging and exciting. Structural remains were identified at the locations of the abbey, icehouse, stables, north and south lodges, and the Doric Temple. These consist of a variety of brick walls, foundations and surfaces, apparently well-preserved. The icehouse, about which very little was previously known, appears to have survived virtually intact. The abbey remains are quite shallow, beneath a thin covering of soil, and the Trust intends to hold a community archaeology event, to enable local people to get their fingernails dirty and help excavate these remains, at the same time uncovering more of the building's secrets. Maybe the 'grey lady' will put in an appearance!

The one disappointment was the complete lack of clues about the location of Warley Tor; excavations revealed only ash and slag landfill material. It is possible the dig was in the wrong place, as the precise location of the Tor has never been confirmed. It is equally feasible, however, that when the building was demolished, around the mid-1800s, materials were re-used and all traces of foundations removed.

In addition to further archaeological investigations, there remain a number of items of work to be carried out before the end of 2007. The main carriage drive will be rebuilt and restored all the way from Lightwoods Hill through to Abbey Road, with a properly surfaced car park provided close to the Abbey road entrance. Steel railings are to be installed along the entire length of Lightwoods Hill and Harborne Road, extending along Abbey Road as far as the driveway. The work will include repairs to the retaining wall along this part of Abbey Road, and there will be gateways and entrances in a sympathetic and matching style. Footpaths will be restored around the winter garden and arboretum; new woodland walks will be created behind the abbey site, and a new, fenced and dog-free play area introduced near the site of the former car park and tennis courts, close to the main drive.

The Trust's guiding philosophy begins with understanding and embracing the design principles established by Humphry Repton two centuries ago. However, there is an acceptance that the way people use public space in the twenty-first century requires a whole range of additional factors to be taken into account when designing and managing a space. Safety and security of park users; accessibility for the less able; preventing unauthorised vehicle access; ensuring that maintenance can be carried out cost-effectively; collection and disposal of litter and dog-mess; securing diversity of plants and animals; managing resources sustainably; and finally health and safety, arising from the operation of a golf course within a public park – these all influence decisions of design, location and materials.

Above all, the park must be safe, enjoyable, accessible and welcoming to all, and should offer a balance between conflicting needs and objectives. To use one example, the main driveway, play area, woodland walks and arboretum/winter garden will offer well-drained, all-weather surfaces and easy gradients, making them suitable for the less mobile, for toddlers and for wheelchairs and buggies. By contrast, most of the paths that run through the woodland near Barclay Road, or around the edge of the golf course by Harborne Road will be surfaced in pebbles or woodchip, largely as now. The informal and less park-like nature of these routes contributes greatly to the sense of wildness and spaciousness that provides Warley Woods with its unique atmosphere.

104 Just one of the problems the Trust has to deal with.

105 A general view of the Trust's well-attended Picnic in the Park.

106 · 107 · 108
From putting up marquees early in the morning, to collecting litter after the crowds have gone home, volunteers have a busy day making the Picnic an enjoyable and successful event.

Look at Warley Woods today, remove some of the more recent tree and shrub planting in the foreground, and in many ways the view from the site of the abbey remains much the same as Repton had intended it to be two centuries ago. It is interesting that now, two hundred years after Repton produced his Red Book, we can experience and enjoy the outcome of his plans, in a way that neither he nor the Galton family ever could. The lesson here is that real landscapes mature and evolve very slowly, a fact that seems lost on those today who demand and expect instant results.

Like Repton, the Trust's vision for restoring the park is unashamedly long term. The landscape of Warley Woods is dominated by features that are both large-scale and slow-growing i.e. trees. The park today could be described as "over-mature". Many of the trees we see around us are veterans, over 150 years old, and some surviving since Repton's time. Amongst these, the elderly beeches in particular are nearing the end of their lives and, with every gale that passes, a few more of them fall over. What the park lacks is a replacement stock of young to middle-aged successors to these ancient trees. Previous guardians of our park failed to plant saplings and young trees 50, 70 and 100 years ago, trees that by now would provide continuity for Repton's landscape vision. Where younger trees do exist, they are often in the wrong places, such as the two groups either side of the meadow that already conflict with, and will eventually undermine, Repton's vistas and planting philosophy. A plantation of young beeches was also established during the 1950s, along the eastern skyline of the park on the site of the former allotments in Barclay Road. Whilst these appear at first glance to have grown well, almost all have in fact been badly damaged by grey squirrel activity, and consequently may not survive to a great age. Perhaps there is a case for restoring the grey squirrel bounty that was offered in the 1950s, when 5 shillings [25 pence] was paid for each tail.

What all this means is that over the next five to thirty years, veteran trees will continue to be lost, and there will inevitably be a timelag before modern successors can take their place. The structure and feel of Warley Woods may well change more radically than at any time over the past century, and in the short term the Trust may struggle to retain the integrity of Repton's inspirational and visionary landscape design.

Whilst this is undoubtedly a daunting challenge, it is one that the Trust is prepared to face up to. The alternative – continuing decline and dereliction, leading to a gradual abandonment of the park amidst a sense of despair and helplessness that nobody cares enough to do anything about it – is unthinkable. Above all, Warley Woods Community Trust is there to represent the community, and to both harness and focus the energies of local people. To be successful, the Trust requires the continued support of a body of local volunteers, each of whom believes sufficiently in the restoration of the woods to commit their time and energy into ensuring this unique project succeeds.

In making this investment, the Trust is setting out to restore and revive the now-faded glories of this still beautiful and charismatic place that has provided successive generations of the public with enjoyment and recreation for a century. In addition, the Trust is focussing on offering a safe, welcoming and attractive green haven for the current generation of park users. Decisions made and actions taken now will ensure that Warley Woods is still around in another hundred years time, meeting the needs of our descendants, and enabling them to make plans of their own to commemorate the bicentenary of 'The People's Park'.

Changing Seasons in Warley Woods

109 Warley Woods has always been a magnet for tobogganists during snowy winters, as seen here in 1952 . . .

110 . . . and again in December 2000.

111 A snowy carriage drive, looking towards Lightwoods Hill in 2001.

113 In January 2003 severe winds brought down a number of trees. Three oaks fell like dominoes across the carriage drive near Lightwoods Hill.

115 The 'occasional' stream in spate, following two cloudbursts: July 2nd 2000.

112 "Where's that ball gone"; a foggy start to a round in February 2006.

114 Exploring a little used path, near the bottom of the golf course, on a rainy afternoon in April 2006.

116 A panorama of Abbey Road School, Barclay Road and a corner of the Woods, taken from the Methodist church tower shortly before its demolition, in 1990.

117 Abbey Road School, seen from what is now Maurice Road, soon after its completion in 1910; it was to be several years before the summit of Abbey Road was reduced and the retaining wall built.

Round and about Warley Woods - Abbey Road

118 The corner of Abbey Road and Pitcairn Road c.1930. The road had been widened and regraded a few years before, enabling these houses to be built.

119 The same scene in 2006: surprisingly little has changed, other than much-improved streetlighting.

120 In 1927 the summits of both hills on Abbey Road were lowered. The retaining wall shows this change in level. After nearly 80 years the wall is now badly in need of repair and plans are being prepared to rebuild it later in 2006.

Round and about Warley Woods - Harborne Road

121 Harborne Road / Pottery Road junction, with the Woods on the right. Construction of new houses was to continue around the corner and down Pottery Road, which at this time appears little more than a country lane.

122 Harborne Road c.1960, with the Woods to the left. The railings around the golf course had been removed as part of the war effort and replaced with a timber paling fence. The Trust intends, with Lottery support, to reinstate the railings.

123 A postcard from the early 1930s, looking up Harborne Road towards the water tower, with railings still in place around the golf course. Although some of the distinctive tall trees on the right have since been lost, a number still remain, and these are visible on the skyline from Birmingham city centre.

124 In 1896, construction began on the Elan aqueduct, to bring water from Wales to serve the city of Birmingham. Since its completion in 1904, water has been pumped from Frankley waterworks to storage reservoirs at high points around the city. One of these is the covered reservoir on top of Warley hill, outside the city boundary; it can be seen beyond the house. The distinctive water tower next to it was built in 1939 by the South Staffordshire water company to supply Smethwick. The water, which largely originates from boreholes, is pumped to the tower from Oldbury.

Round and about Warley Woods - Barclay Road

125 The corner of Lightwoods Hill and Barclay Road, in 1936; the original park railings remain in place here.

126 Lots of detail in this atmospheric pre-First World War postcard of newly-built houses in Barclay Road. Not a single car to be seen, just a couple of horses and carts in the distance. Note the varied styles of front boundary walls, also the rough timber paling fence along the edge of the woods. People moved here to enjoy the fresh air, which might explain the number of open windows. The original caption "Barclay Road, Bearwood" has been erased and overprinted.

127 The same view, in 2006. Many more cars, of course; much better street lighting and the fencing to the woods has gone. Otherwise, little has changed.

The Grey Lady - and other mysteries

Mention Warley Abbey to most people and, irrespective of their age, conversation soon comes around the ghost of the 'Grey Lady'. In many ways it is entirely to be expected that such a legend should grow up over the years; an isolated hall, gloomy forbidding and spooky, set alone amongst the trees in its own parkland has all the right ingredients for a good ghost tale.

The first reference to the Grey Lady dates from 1888, during Sir Hugh Gilzean-Reid's occupation of Warley. Late one evening, towards the end of a dinner party, it is reported that the lights turned blue, there was a knocking at the door, then the door opened as if by itself and a grey lady was seen "with hands uplifted and head thrown backing a dramatic attitude". Amazingly, this apparition stayed long enough for one of the guests, Harry Furniss, to sketch the scene. Suffice to say, Gilzean-Reid was in the newspaper business, and clearly had a nose for a good story.

Some years later, when George Bretherick and his family were sole occupiers of the abbey, his sons attended Abbey Road Schools, and apparently did much to keep the legend of the grey lady alive. Schoolfriends were invited back to play in the largely uninhabited abbey, and, after the gates had been locked, the equally deserted park. To most children of an impressionable age this was a suitably spooky setting, and by all accounts the junior Brethericks rose to the occasion, by luring young visitors into the extensive cellars beneath the abbey, and staging their very own haunting.

Rumours persisted for many years about a tunnel supposedly connecting Warley with Halesowen Abbey – some say it was Dudley Castle, while others still believe this to be true. What is certain is that in addition to the cellars beneath the abbey, there was also a mysterious entrance, leading down some steps from the courtyard, near the stables. The steps led to a bricked-up doorway, and there was a further entrance covered by an iron grating. Needless to say, these features, together with the former icehouse [known to some as 'the crypt'] became the source of continued intrigue and speculation.

The abbey was demolished almost 50 years ago, and no obvious traces remain, yet to this day the legend of the "grey lady of Warley Woods" lives on amongst local children. Now, if only the archaeology dig could uncover that tunnel to Halesowen . . .

128 'The Grey Lady':
an original drawing by David Yates

If reading any part of this book prompts you to share additional stories, memories or photographs, particularly relating to the more recent history of Warley Woods, we would love to hear from you.

Please contact the Trust at:

Warley Woods Community Trust
The Pavilion
Lightwoods Hill
Smethwick
West Midlands
B67 5ED

Telephone 0121 420 1061

email: admin@warleywoods.org.uk

www.warleywoods.org.uk

"This is the completion of a great scheme, which should prove to the inestimable benefit of generations to come. You see around you a beautiful park which, in the course of time, had it not been secured, must undoubtedly become a mass of bricks and mortar"

Councillor A Reynolds, Lord Mayor, 1906

"Warley Woods was a fabulous place to play when I was growing up – like being in a 'Just William' story"

Geoff Gray, Local Resident, 2006